Who Killed Ben Miller?

D. A. FEATHERLING

DEDICATION

To the team who helped research the stories — you guys are the best!

ACKNOWLEDGMENTS

There are many people who helped in preparing this manuscript who must be acknowledged.

First, Weldon, Roy, and Bill – you guys have been a tremendous help and inspiration throughout this process. Thanks to Lieutenant Mike Cowie of the Williamson County Sheriff's Office, Criminal Investigations Division for research assistance. Also Jennifer Smith, Crime Scene Specialist, for discussions about murder scenes.

Various people in city, county and state offices, libraries, and organizations who were more than helpful. I appreciate it.

Folks who provided information to assist the project with the facts as they knew them. Bless you for sharing.

Bo Stearns and Scott Perkins, my knights-of-the-road, who pulled me from a ditch.

Beta readers, Peggy Caravantes, Lin Harris, and Linda Helms...your comments always make a difference and thanks for brainstorming help, too.

Last, but most importantly, to my Lord and Savior, Jesus Christ, without whom I would never be able to do what I do.

AUTHOR FOREWORD

I tried not to write this book.

I really did.

When first approached by Weldon Mersiovsky, an area historian/genealogist about two stories — one involving an unsolved murder and another an unusual death of a juror — they sounded interesting, but I write fiction, including mysteries, but not non-fiction.

However, I agreed to talk with the people who had the information about the stories within the next few weeks.

I later met with one of them about the 1930 cold case murder. Roy Headrick had been gathering information for over ten years. His notes and account of the case were intriguing to a mystery buff, and I went home with a brown envelope stuffed full of old newspaper clippings and information he'd gathered.

After reviewing everything, it was apparent much more research would need to be done for the story to be as complete as possible. I didn't think I had the kind of time available to do the job right, but I thought, I prayed, I thought some more.

With regret, I told Roy I would have to pass on the project, but gave him some ideas on how the book/research could be accomplished and even suggested a non-fiction writer as a possible contact.

Over the next couple of weeks, though, I could not get the details of the story out of my mind. I started forming sentences to use as lead-ins to chapters, thought of questions needing to be asked, imagined possible answers. It got to the point no matter what I was doing, I was thinking about the murder.

About that time, I kept an appointment with the second person, Henry W. Schkade, Jr. Bill had a family member's death as a juror story to tell. I should say here neither of these gentlemen felt they had the skills to write the books even though they were passionate about the stories being told or they would have done so.

After our discussion, I could see a dearth of information pending on his story as well, but there were also possibilities because of the uniqueness of the event.

I gave in. Called Roy Headrick and agreed I would write the book; told Bill Schkade I would do the same for his story. As a result, this volume birthed with two intriguing stories, both set in the early thirties (BTW, I also don't write historicals), containing all of the drama, intrigue, and suspense any mystery writer could want.

Small towns are, of course, notorious for everyone knowing everyone else's business. Most people would agree with that.

I have found small town citizens can also be exceptionally close-mouthed when they don't want/intend to talk about something. There seems to be a strong concern among the older generations about discussing subjects not previously public knowledge.

In today's world, of course, nothing is private (whether fortunate or unfortunate, let the reader be the judge). Information is shared via the Internet or through electronic devices and email as freely as gossip used to be shared via the telephone party line or in person.

When a particular mystery — provocatively called 'cold cases' these days — has never been solved — after eighty-four years, it has been amazing to see how difficult it can be to get people to provide information. The reasons for this may be many: cultural, relational, or simply a strong sense of self-preservation.

All said to explain that tracking down information after eighty-four years has been difficult, and in some cases, impossible.

Unfortunately, most official records of investigating agencies have been purged and destroyed. Persons living at the time of the crime are few so first-hand memories are lost. Newspaper accounts are sparse as one would expect in a small town, and the flowery style of yesteryear writing is often difficult to interpret or trust.

As a result, information is, in many cases, second or third generation 'hearsay' and therefore may not be a totally accurate depiction of facts. Nevertheless, an argument can be made if enough people tell the same story there is probably some degree of truth involved.

No intent exists on the part of the author to do anything other than tell a story – relating facts where they exist, suppositions where they do not. I have taken the liberty of fictionalizing some sections of both stories based on facts or information. Where I've been given conflicting information about the same situation or character I've taken the liberty of choosing which interpretation to use. The result is questions posed which will let the reader draw their own conclusions about 'whodunit' or 'what really happened.'

But we all do that anyway, don't we?

D. A. Featherling
Georgetown, Texas
November 21, 2014

CHAPTER 1

THE CRIME

September 8, 1930

Ben whistled softly between his teeth as he steered the car toward home. The cool early morning breeze blew through the windows of his Model A Roadster, calmed his emotions.

He always hated to leave Ola Mae at her home and go his separate way. He could only hope their long engagement would soon end in marriage. Then they would have their own home and be together forever.

As he drove from Georgetown toward the turnoff to Walburg, his thoughts kept pace with the turning wheels. He grinned, winced as his nose twinged at the sudden movement of facial muscles. He touched the broken bone gingerly. Thanks, Georgetown gang. His nose, and some assorted bruises and sore ribs, recalled his fight in the park with them a week ago.

He'd been minding his own business, strolling through San Gabriel Park with several of Ola Mae's brothers. He'd hoped by getting to know them better they'd be even more in favor of their only sister marrying a German-American.

Ben knew his Lutheran background offended many in the community of Georgetown. There was a lot of mistrust between the German community in Walburg and the residents of Georgetown, a few miles away. Since Ola Mae had been taking instruction in the Missouri branch of the Lutheran church so they could marry in the church, he'd been concerned her family might hold her conversion against him.

Guess he should have stayed away from her brothers, but he hadn't and they'd headed toward the bath house and Ben's car. At least they enjoyed riding in his car.

The appearance of the Georgetown gang – Loss Sudduth, Red Williams, and Burrell Gunn – had taken all of them by surprise. Ben would have pushed on past and kept walking, but the words and slurs about him, and especially Ola Mae, didn't take long for him to get mad and a fight to begin.

He'd held his own, if he did say so himself. He grinned, this time a bit more carefully, as he recalled one particularly well-placed punch to Loss's bulging midriff.

Marvin Edwards had erupted from the bath house where he was staying nights and tried to break up the melee after he heard the bad language being used. Eventually he prevailed, especially when he told them it was almost time for local law enforcement to make a check of the park.

The gang scattered, and Ben and Ola Mae's brothers hot-footed it to the car and got on the road before they encountered the Sheriff's Department.

That little brawl had been the reason he and Ola Mae spent Sunday, now yesterday, forty miles north in Temple. After the park incident, Ben wasn't sure if they'd be safe if they were found alone by the Georgetown gang. He knew he couldn't defend Ola Mae and himself against three of them. Especially if Red Williams pulled a knife which he was prone to do.

Ben shook his head, cringed again at the pain.

Ow. He had to stop doing that.

The moon showed high, shedding light every time a cloud allowed it freedom from cover. He'd be home soon. Perhaps he could convince Ola Mae they should be married when she finished her church instruction in another week or two. The Georgetown gang had threatened months ago that Ben might go with Ola Mae, but he'd never marry her.

His lips thinned. He'd marry her all right and there was nothing the gang could do to stop them. It would be easy enough, if they had to, to go to Belton and get a marriage license and have the ceremony there or another small town, although it would be nice to have a typical German wedding and celebration to welcome her to the Miller family.

Thinking of German traditions brought Edd to his mind. Little Edna Zingelmann, his former girlfriend. His dating Edd had met with the approval of their families. Not that there was much left of Ben's family. His parents were dead, his residence with his brother

Martin's family, had been a huge blessing when he'd been left on his own. All his brothers and sisters would welcome Ola Mae even though they'd been fond of Edd.

He'd hated hurting the young girl when he cut off their relationship. But how could you help yourself when you fell in love with the most beautiful girl in the world? A sigh slipped from between his lips.

His mind skipped to the night at the Behrensville Rifle Club dance in Theon, Texas. He'd gone there, as did many of the young Walburgers, to socialize with other single young people. Edd hadn't felt well so he'd gone alone.

Good thing. He'd only been there a few minutes, was scanning the crowd to see who he knew and might go talk to, when he'd spotted a blonde-haired, blue-eyed beauty — Ola Mae Kimbro. Of course, at the time, he didn't know her name. He only knew when his glance met hers, there was a magnetic force that drew them toward each other from opposite sides of the room.

They met in the middle of the dance floor, gazed deeply into each other's eyes. The next thing he knew they were dancing, although he didn't remember asking or her accepting.

The evening flew by. When the dance was over, his murmured "May I take you home?" was answered with one swift nod. They'd left the dance and headed to Georgetown along the road leading to the North Town area where Ola Mae lived.

That overwhelming love at first sight on both their

parts had been the beginning of their relationship. Ola Mae was the love of his life — quiet, sweet, but appealing in every way. He'd never known anyone like her.

His conscience twinged, as it had done several times since he'd had to tell Edd they wouldn't be going together anymore. He knew she'd assumed they would marry someday. They'd dated nearly two years and his family and hers had accepted the match as a fact. Sweet little Edd. He'd hated to hurt her, but he'd known he could never marry anyone but Ola Mae.

The passage of a cloud in front of the moon brought him out of his reverie. He'd better pay attention to his driving. This was no time to have a wreck and damage his new car – his pride and joy. Or to injure himself. Not if there was to be a wedding soon. A broken nose was bad enough.

Home was only a few miles further. At least it would be late enough when he reached the turnoff he shouldn't run into the party going on earlier at the Dry Berry Creek Bridge. He'd steered around the group of boys and girls when he and Ola Mae drove to her house.

The group was sitting around on the bridge as they often did, smoking and probably drinking, too. Ben had eased his car past them on the bridge, responded with nods and waves to their yelled greetings and invitations to stop.

Since it was now after one o'clock in the morning, they should all be gone and he'd have the road to himself. He didn't want to encounter any of the Georgetown gang again if they were still there. Especially if the bootleg liquor had been flowing as freely as it usually did at one of the get-togethers.

His thoughts drifted again to Ola Mae and the last few kisses they'd shared. She'd teased him about his slender mustache and how it tickled her upper lip.

Oops. There was the bridge ahead. He needed to get his mind off his love life and be prepared for the left turn downward from the higher level of the road. If you hit that drop off too quick, you'd really get a jar.

He stuck out his arm automatically to signal. Unnecessary since there was no traffic, but it was a good habit to have. A quick glance as he made the left assured him the bridge party had ended and he was alone.

Ben eased the car from the road onto the gravel pathway and steered the car slowly. Just a short way to reach the creek and enter it for the rest of the journey. Alert now he concentrated on his driving, not his thoughts.

Headlight beams reflected an obstacle in front of him. He slammed the brakes against the floorboard. The rear of the car shimmied as he came to a sudden halt.

Why was a car stopped on the path?

Uh, oh. Red Williams stood silhouetted against the black backdrop of trees, ground, and the bulk of another vehicle.

Perhaps Ben could outtalk him, but he didn't dare leave the car to do it. Williams might take the vehicle or damage it and Ben couldn't afford that.

Williams didn't move, one arm around a sagging figure at his side. Another person stood to the right, also grasping the man in the middle as they held him upright. Please, not Loss Sudduth. A sinking feeling welled up in his gut.

"Hey."

Williams' voice echoed in the night as his huge bear-like figure loomed in front of the car.

"Give us a hand."

It was more a demand than a request.

Ben stayed still, his thoughts darted here and there as he tried to figure how to get away from what could be a dangerous situation, depending on what Williams wanted, and the man's level of drunkenness. The guy was all too willing to pull a knife.

With relief, Ben realized the third person wasn't Sudduth, but a stranger. Who was the man wearing the cowboy hat? He'd never seen him before.

As they dragged their burden, approached the front of the car, Ben automatically reached in his shirt pocket for his pack of smokes. He pulled a cigarette out and placed it between his lips, fumbled for a match.

Williams' voice sounded again. "Give us a hand with Gunn."

Burrell Gunn. He wasn't too bad. Maybe it would be all right. Maybe he could give them all a ride to North Town. It was only a few miles back. Then he'd be done and could go to his own home. He had to get up early the next morning to make it on time to his telephone lineman job.

He drew a deep breath, struck the match, applied the flame to the tip of his cigarette. He heard what sounded like an explosion and his head rocked from a sudden blow. The cigarette fell from his mouth.

He tried to turn, but something was wrong.

Pain hit him in waves. He vaguely sensed someone on the passenger side of the car. What were they pointing at him?

The still flaming match slipped from fingers gone nerveless and limp.

"I told you she'd never marry you."

The voice came from far away. Light and dark flashed in kaleidoscopic patterns in his mind. Another explosion – another blow to the side of his head.

Then…nothing.

****

Less than an hour had passed since Ben Miller left Ola Mae Kimbro at her home at 1:15 a.m., Monday, September 8, 1930.

Two gunshot wounds to the head set the stage for a mystery not solved in 1930. A mystery still unsolved eighty-four years later.

The question still remains.

Who killed Ben Miller?

CHAPTER 2

THE LOCALE

Georgetown, Texas is located on the northeastern edge of what is known as the Texas Hill Country. The North and Middle Forks of the San Gabriel River both run through the city.

The year 1930 saw a town divided into unofficial segments – those more of finance and class than geography. The people who lived north of town were primarily white...poor whites, in very, very modest little homes. They were called "Charcoal Burners" since the area contained lots of cedar trees. They sold the charcoal to people who ironed clothes for a living. The wood was used to heat their irons since such appliances weren't electric during those days.

The people who lived on farms, and many had big farms, were called "Brush Burners." The farm's soil was so poor it wouldn't grow cotton or good vegetables so all they could do was raise goats and sheep.

The Southwestern University area was called

Methodist Town. A lot of moneyed people lived there. The Ridge (or Negro Ridge as it was called in 1930) was below where the I&GN railroad tracks used to be. The affluent people lived on the east side and the blacks on the Ridge. Some whites lived in what was known as Grasshopper Town (North Town). It was on the west side between the Ridge and the affluent part of town.

Most of the persons mentioned in this book lived in North Town, that area north of the San Gabriel River. It was outside of the Georgetown city limits. Residents had little to do with the city since city services and utilities were not furnished to North Town. In fact, most North Towners still had outhouses rather than indoor plumbing, even into the fifties.

One man, related to the Glasscock family (big landowners), had a water line which the North Town residents could use. They either bought water from him or dug their own well.

The area had no form of organized government and was simply an independent settlement where poor people lived.

Although residents of North Town grew up during Prohibition, alcohol was readily available. Georgetown itself was dry. The city of Walburg supplied liquor to those in the area who wanted alcohol (beer). Bootleggers were also extremely active during the time.

In North Town during the twenties, thirties, and throughout the forties and even beyond, everyone maintained a garden. Many had chickens, pigs, and cows as well.

People who lived in North Town during those days remember there being lots of gravy, cornbread, and biscuits at every meal. Sometimes one or more of those items were the entire meal.

North Town was considered to be on a lower socio-economic level than Georgetown. In the thirties it wasn't unusual for people to go to work on city streets or county roads to earn money to pay their bills.

North Town did not become a part of Georgetown for many years.

****

Since some of the people involved in the murder were from Walburg, Texas, the community's existence also demands some explanation.

The town was never huge, population-wise. The ethnic groups represented by the settlers included Germans, Wendish, Czechoslovakian, Austrian, and Swiss. There were probably fewer than 100 people living there at the time of the murder.

In the 1930's, Walburg and Georgetown were comprised of very different cultures. People in Georgetown were a mix of backgrounds. They had been in the area longer and represented many different faiths and ethnic groups. The people in Walburg were mainly German and mostly of the Lutheran religion.

The Georgetown folks didn't want a Georgetown young man dating a Lutheran girl from Walburg (and vice versa). It was frowned upon by both groups.

One resident stated the German people in Walburg wanted their children to marry other Germans. The Georgetown people didn't care about the religious differences, but the Walburg people did.

****

The year 1930 was an interesting one. Americans were still in the midst of a depression...known as the "Great Depression."

Even though Georgetown and Williamson County in general, later recovered their economies, there were still many residents in the area who were 'dirt poor' in the thirties, a situation which lasted a decade or more. Prohibition was also still in effect.

In interviewing a number of persons about this story, most mentioned the hard times existing in 1930.

They also referred to several of the persons involved in this story as being 'mean', or 'no good.' It was repeated so often it sounded as though most of the population of Georgetown and North Town at the time was full of folks who were of questionable reputation.

Whether or not the perception was true, the details of the case certainly make it sound possible.

CHAPTER 3

THE BACKGROUND

The murder of 21-year-old Ben Miller took place on a lonely country pathway in a post-World War I society, a country in the midst of a Depression, one still under the law of prohibition.

The case, though investigated according to newspaper accounts by the Williamson County Sheriff's Department with assists from the State Highway Patrol (Texas Rangers), produced no suspects, no arrests, and no one local was ever questioned.

In fact, a *San Antonio Express* article stated "Officers are positive no personal enemy killed the young farmer and that the motive was to secure the car."

The Sheriff's Department claimed to be unaware of the feud between Ben and the Georgetown gang until the gun used to commit the murder was found later.

A review of information from many local sources

is required to try to understand the motive for killing Ben Miller and to try to determine who pulled the trigger.

****

Ben Miller was born on November 22, 1908 in Williamson County, Texas, to Henry and Marie Miller. He had six brothers and one living sister. Ben was next to the youngest of the siblings.

He was nineteen years old when his mother died several years after his father. Ben went to live with his brother Martin Miller's family. There were two parents, two children, and Ben living in a four-room bungalow house in Walburg. He lived with them until the day of his death.

Ben was a handsome young man, clean-living, and quite popular with the young ladies. Not only did Ben have looks and charm, but he owned a new maroon 1930 Model A Ford Roadster convertible. When Ben drove along the street, the canvas top lowered on his car, with his black hair and dark eyes, all the girls watched. There was room in the car for a rumble seat, but Ben didn't have the extra seventy-five dollars to have one installed when he originally bought the vehicle.

Ben worked as a lineman for the telephone company, first in San Antonio, Texas, then returned to the Georgetown/Walburg area after his initial hiring and training in the Alamo City. He always seemed to have plenty of spending money. Since he also worked on the family farm, he was designated in the newspaper stories concerning his death as a farmer.

After meeting Ola Mae Kimbro Ben apparently led a contented life. He and Ola Mae were planning their wedding after dating for a year or so. Besides his job and spending time with Ola Mae, he enjoyed taking his car and his young nephew to Dry Berry Creek where the water was only about three or four inches deep and washing the car frequently as new car owners are prone to do.

The incident at San Gabriel Park was the first indicator of any overt trouble with the Georgetown gang or with anyone else. But after that, Ben's life was never the same.

One can imagine the resentment brewing in the minds of the gang members, who believed Ben had no business dating Ola Mae — they thought she belonged to a man named Loss Sudduth.

Loss was a chubby young man without any special appeal to redeem his appearance and no charm or personality that would draw women to him.

Ola Mae lived, and Loss visited friends frequently, on the same street north of the San Gabriel River in the area known as "North Town." It was home to poor families who didn't live in the city of Georgetown. Since the North Town residents all lived close to each other, everyone knew everyone else, and in many cases the families were related by marriage.

It is not difficult to believe that the young man growing up, being exposed on a daily basis to Ola Mae, often designated "the prettiest girl in Georgetown," would have feelings for her. Even though there was a four-year difference in their ages (Ola Mae was older), the young man may have had one of those passionate crushes young people in their teens often experience.

As Ben made his frequent drives through North Town, with all the girls watching him and envying Ola Mae, it's not hard to imagine the jealous thoughts of a would-be suitor on the sidelines.

****

As mentioned before, Ben and Ola Mae met at the Behrensville Rifle Club (pronounced Burnsville) in Theon, Texas. It was located about a half mile west of where the Possum Creek Inn is now. The Behrensville club only provided an opportunity for young people to meet potential mates. They had dances and singles would go there on Sunday evenings and shoot in competitions. In a rural area, there was little to do socially, and this club (and similar ones) provided an opportunity for the young people to get together.

The club was similar to one located in Walburg. The Walburg Club supposedly had secret meetings as did the Masons and other groups. The Theon club was evidently more for singles from Walburg than those from Georgetown.

As a result, when Georgetown young people crashed the dances, they weren't wanted and feathers were ruffled. The separateness of the towns of Georgetown and Walburg had a huge impact on the area in this, and many other ways.

Ola Mae was at the Behrensville club one night, reportedly with Loss Sudduth and his two gang members – Red Williams and Burrell Gunn.

Even though Williams and Gunn were both in their twenties at the time, they evidently followed seventeen-year-old Loss as their leader and probably took their cues from him as to what would comprise an evening's entertainment. Since the most aggressive one was related to him by marriage, they may have allowed Loss to be the 'head.'

Different accounts state Ola Mae was there with the gang – or she and another girl were there with them – and still another version says two other girls and another young man were there with her, as well as the gang.

Regardless of who was there, it's not hard to imagine the encounter:

Behrensville Rifle Club, 1930
Ola Mae Kimbro sashayed through the door of the Behrensville club in Walburg. She looked good tonight

and she knew it. Oh, people didn't think she knew what they said about her, but she did. She had to admit, she rather liked being designated as the 'prettiest girl in Georgetown.'

She tossed her curls. She'd taken special pains to enhance her appearance for this evening. She could tell by the sideways glances from the young men present she'd accomplished her goal.

A look to her left caused her a half frown. Too bad she didn't have someone more exciting than Loss Sudduth and his relatives to escort her. But, maybe the other people at the dance wouldn't know one of the men was married, and think she was even more desirable since she had so many men with her.

She heaved a silent sigh. Why couldn't someone have asked her to the dance who was even half as exciting as the cowboy heroes who peopled the Westerns she read every day? That's what she wanted. Someone handsome and slightly dangerous. Her lip curled without conscious thought. Loss certainly didn't meet the criteria – although he might be considered dangerous considering some of the activities she'd heard he was involved in.

Never mind. She'd been bored with sitting at home again on a Friday night. Being young and pretty, she needed to get out and enjoy herself. Besides, if she didn't meet other people, how would she ever find her one true love?

She knew he was out there somewhere. She'd decided her reputation could suffer through one evening with Loss and his gang if it gained her a hero in return.

Half an hour later, a glass of soda finished, she banged the empty glass on the bar behind her. The music played on.

"Wantta dance?"

Loss' voice interrupted her disappointed thoughts.

"No, thanks."

"I thought you came to dance."

His persistence irritated her.

"I did."

"You can dance with me. I'm not an old married man like Red."

"Not right now."

"Fine."

Loss sounded sulky, turned away from her toward his buddies, Red Williams and Burrell Gunn.

Good. Perhaps he'd decide to take her home early.

So far, no one had approached her for a dance. It may have had something to do with the reputation she'd heard Loss had. Now she believed it. The other men present must be afraid. She sneaked a sideways look at him.

Short, pudgy, little hair. Ugh. Not her cup of tea. She wanted…no, she needed…a man like…a man like…him.

She caught her breath as she spotted the young man standing by the door. He'd evidently just entered, because she certainly hadn't seen him before.

Tall, nicely dressed, black, black hair, dark eyes, and a pencil-slim mustache. Add a scarf at his neck, and a Stetson pushed back on his head and he'd be the hero of her dreams.

He turned his head toward her. Their glances caught, held.

Without conscious thought, her eyes fastened on him and she started walking across the room.

"Hey, Ola Mae, where you goin'?"

She ignored Loss's question and kept walking toward the man she knew was her destiny.

He walked as surely toward her.

When they reached the middle of the dance floor, they stopped, as though commanded to do so.

He gazed deeply into her eyes, smiled, held out his arms.

Without any more of an invitation, she slipped into them and they began to move to the music.

Time flew by. They danced every dance without words. Sometimes they would simply gaze at each other – an experience that reached to her soul. Her heart pounded and her breath came in ragged spurts.

He stopped. She realized the music had, too.

"May I take you home?"

She nodded.

He could take her anywhere. Her life was melded to his now and there would be no turning back.

Ola Mae Kimbro knew her dream had just become reality.

****

The meeting between Ola Mae and Ben is highly reminiscent of the lyrics to the song, "Some Enchanted Evening" — as fulfilling an encounter as any romantic young woman could wish.

Ben and Ola Mae's preoccupation with only each other that evening and afterward probably generated the ill feelings later showed and eventually acted upon by the killer.

CHAPTER 4

THE INVESTIGATION

Monday, September 8, 1930, at about six a.m., Williamson County officers were notified the body of a man had been seen lying by the side of the south approach to Dry Berry Creek Bridge.

The *Williamson County Sun* reported that Herman Kelm, a resident of Walburg, was on his way to Georgetown when he spotted the body on the embankment.

However, the *Temple Daily Telegram* stated the body was found by Newt Purcell and M. Tolland, farmers on their way to Georgetown; therefore it is unclear who actually reported the crime.

Deputy Sheriff B. M. McLaughlin, Justice C. R. Faubion, County Attorney D. B. Wood and others immediately went to the scene and found Ben Miller's body.

After viewing the remains, Faubion ordered the body turned over to the undertaker. It was removed to their parlors, where it was supposedly viewed by hundreds during the morning.

Two bullet wounds were in the right side of the head, indicating Miller had been fired upon from the passenger side of the car as he sat at the steering wheel. His body was thrown onto the embankment by the path and the car stolen. Death was instantaneous, according to Dr. J. G. Whigham, who made a post-mortem examination at the morgue.

Justice Faubion rendered a verdict of death by gunshot wounds at the hands of an assailant or assailants unknown. Faubion also stated one pocket of Miller's trousers was turned wrong side out, indicating he had been robbed. No other valuables were missing.

Two one-dollar bills and some small change were later found at the undertaking parlor in the watch pocket of the trousers.

There is no newspaper mention of Sheriff Louis H. Lowe appearing on the scene at the beginning phases of the investigation.

Officers offered two early theories about Miller's death. One was he picked up a hitchhiker as he drove home after dropping off his fiancée. The other was he was halted as he made the turn onto the side road before the bridge and was murdered there.

It was theorized the car was standing still when the murder was committed since there was no sign it was in motion. If it had been, given the steep incline of the path toward the creek, the car would either have overturned or ended up in the creek with a dead driver at the steering wheel. A heavy rain in the area on the preceding Wednesday should also have left easily identifiable tracks if the car had been moving at random.

Officers immediately notified all surrounding county and city officers, and by noon Monday, the murder had been broadcast to all sections of Texas and adjoining states. Dozens of local officers (perhaps a newspaper exaggeration of how many 'local officers' were actually available? Or perhaps they meant officers throughout the state) spent the day working on clues without any results.

The investigation did show the individual(s) who took Miller's car passed through Granger, Texas about 2:00 o'clock Monday morning, purchased a small amount of gasoline, and asked directions to Hearne, Texas.

It was believed there was a companion inside the car since the driver was heard talking to someone while the garage operator was getting change. Officers theorized another person was hidden in the rumble seat space inside the car.

During the day Monday, Sheriff Louis Lowe posted a $250 reward for the arrest of the killer, and notified officers in surrounding counties to be on the lookout for Miller's car, Texas license number 1-204-239.

On September 14th, the *San Antonio Express*

reported that Governor Dan Moody, at the request of the Miller family, also offered a $250 reward for the killers. One historian stated it was not particularly unusual at that time for the Governor to offer such rewards for crimes committed, so Miller's family probably didn't have any special influence that made it happen.

Late Monday afternoon, the Sheriff's Department was notified the abandoned car had been found soon after daylight at Alvarado, Texas. Alvarado is ten miles south of Fort Worth at the junction of two highways, one leading to Fort Worth, and the other to Dallas and Greenville.

They theorized the murderer, or someone acting for him, had driven the car there and abandoned it before daylight to avoid discovery.

A newspaper article in the *Alvarado Bulletin*, dated September 12, 1930, states the car was evidently driven directly north on Highway No. 2, since it was recovered in Alvarado a short distance from the main highway, where the side road runs west from near the Jack Maddox place past the Carl Laramore place.

Area resident Jess Manis discovered the vehicle where it had been abandoned and he in turn notified the authorities. A Constable Turpen took charge and notified Georgetown police of its discovery.

A man named Bunk Pruitt reported to Turpen that he met a man walking on the highway who fit the description of the wanted driver of the car. The man was seen again near Duncanville. He was reported to be of tall stature and wore boots.

When the Sheriff's Department received the car information, they notified North Texas cities and law enforcement departments. Two Williamson County deputies left early that night for Alvarado and went to Dallas and nearby cities where they gave local law enforcement agencies as much information as they had and asked for their aid.

The State Highway Patrol (Texas Rangers) was supposedly also put to work on the case. A San Antonio newspaper account names Sgt. J. B. Wheatley and Highway Patrolman Jim McCoy as the Rangers assigned to the case. Unfortunately, due to purging of old agency records, the notes on the Miller case have long since been destroyed, as have those of all other law enforcement agencies involved. Therefore, no records are available of any of the official investigation.

Either a few months or a year later (the time frame is unclear), it was reported a couple was on their way to church one Sunday morning. They had driven under the Dry Berry Creek Bridge and were about to get onto the main road leading to Georgetown when they saw a gun hanging in a tree.

They stopped the car and after some discussion brought the gun to town and turned it in to the Sheriff's Office. The tree was in almost the exact location where Ben was killed and supposedly would give the law a new direction to go with the investigation. Unsure if it was the gun used in the murder, the authorities paid two Walburg residents to dig up Ben Miller's body. The two bullets were removed from Miller's head.

The gun, a .25 automatic, was taken to Austin (one presumes to Ranger or Highway Patrol headquarters) and fired into a sandbag. The bullets were retrieved and compared to those taken from Miller's head. They were a match.

Unfortunately, the gun and the bullets, although reported by one source as once having been seen in the Courthouse, disappeared and were never found.

Another source reported when the murder gun was first found Burrell Gunn claimed it and said it had been stolen from his car on Saturday night while parked on the Georgetown square. Nothing substantiates his story and it is presumed the source had the wrong name attached to the gun as detailed in a later chapter.

In mid- September of the year Ben was killed, an article in the *San Antonio Express*, dated September 14th, stated a man and a woman were arrested in Tyler as suspects in Miller's murder. Sheriff Louis Lowe and deputies brought them to Georgetown.

After several hours of interrogation, they were released from custody. The couple was able to give a reasonable account of themselves for the week preceding the murder and on the day of and day after the crime.

They were nowhere close to the scene when the killing occurred.

The same article mentions that the following day, after questioning the couple, officers went from Georgetown to Bellville where another couple was being held. They questioned them but found they were not involved in the crime.

It is unknown why couples were targeted in the investigation unless it was a red herring to keep investigators off the real trail until enough time had passed to declare the case unsolved.

Interestingly enough, the *Alvarado Bulletin*, in a September 12, 1930 article, does mention the driver of Miller's abandoned car in Alvarado was thought to have had a woman with him, at least part of the trip.

Another article in the *San Antonio Express*, dated September 20, 1930, stated that a man was held in jail on September 19th for investigation in connection with the murder of Ben Miller.

The man was arrested by Constable Roy Holman of Round Rock when the man was unable to give a satisfactory account of his whereabouts the night of the slaying. Officers said he fitted the description of the man seen in Miller's car at Granger.

Nothing further was ever heard, so presumably the man was released and not considered a serious suspect after more questioning.

An ending paragraph in the newspaper article

stated during the three weeks after the murder, local, county, precinct, city officers, rangers, and others investigated and supposedly obtained many clues, yet with no arrest being made.

Clues that were going to lead to the arrest of the guilty parties were unearthed, according to the newspaper, but officers declined to reveal them to keep from interfering with the investigation.

If this level of involvement was actually correct, those clues either led nowhere, or were the product of a reporter's vivid imagination.

One other story found in a newspaper dated March, 1931, detailed the arrest of three youths in Minnesota for burglary.

Investigators found the young men, all under the age of twenty, had robbed a service station in Bell County on February 13th. The owner interrupted the crime and was shot.

The story indicated it was hoped the men could be tied to the Ben Miller murder, since they were in the Georgetown area during the time of Miller's killing.

No further information was ever printed, but the story stated the youths were returned to Minnesota for prosecution of burglaries committed there, so there was evidently no connection to the Miller case.

One more fruitless lead.

Louis Lowe and his staff were kept fairly busy for a month or so after the murder following up clues sent by other investigating agencies and law enforcement officers who were trying to help.

CHAPTER 5

THE INVESTIGATORS

The primary information about the investigations into Ben Miller's death is drawn from various newspaper accounts. Information about those who either investigated the crime, or who were supposed to have done so, is even sparser.

Louis H. Lowe - At the time of the murder, Louis H. Lowe was the Sheriff of Williamson County. He was 61 years old in 1930 and served as sheriff until 1936. Lowe was in law enforcement at some level for fifty-seven years.

Lowe was not well-regarded in the community and was known for behavior which some thought inappropriate for an officer of the law. One source reported Lowe would go to gatherings, get drunk, then pick up someone on the road and harass them as he drove. Lowe was reported to be a heavy drinker. The feeling was Lowe didn't represent his profession as he should at any time.

Once, Lowe went to a beer joint in Walburg. He was going to arrest a drunken woman. A soldier drinking there volunteered for Lowe to take him to jail rather than the woman. He was ignored. He repeated the offer. Lowe took his gun and slashed the soldier across the face with it. While dramatic, either the soldier had a gun or the story is exaggerated since Lowe reportedly didn't carry a gun.

Deputy Berney McLaughlin and Constable Turpen - Ben's abandoned car was taken to the Reese Bros. Garage in Alvarado by a Constable Turpen who took charge of the vehicle. Turpen also notified Georgetown police about the car. Deputy Berney McLaughlin of Williamson County was sent to Alvarado to get it Tuesday afternoon. For some reason he had the car washed, greased, and the oil changed. Was it to get rid of any blood inside the car? Why would the law not have left such evidence intact?

According to a present-day crime scene investigator, even though Miller's wounds would not have bled much initially because of the small caliber of gun used, when the body was removed from the vehicle, a good deal of blood would have been expelled during the process.

Did the deputy not want to ride in a bloody car? Or had he been instructed to get rid of any stains? Again, the *Alvarado Bulletin* newspaper article stated the Constable who took charge of the vehicle said there were a few blood drops on the car, indicating Miller was shot at close range, probably as he sat in the machine. Investigators on the scene had already made that determination as well.

McLaughlin complied with his orders and the car was returned to Georgetown to the Miller family.

Martin Miller, the brother with whom Ben resided, had to pay for the car being cleaned even though it was done without his consent or by his request.

The Texas Rangers – The Rangers were also involved in investigating the Miller murder. According to a newspaper article in the *San Antonio Express*, dated September 14, 1930, Ranger Sergeant J. B. Wheatley and Patrolman Jim McCoy were put on the case. A private investigator was also employed later, but records from both those sources have been lost or destroyed.

A Texas Ranger named Fred Olson from Round Rock came into the picture much later. Martin Miller met Olson and told him the murder investigation had been botched. Olson started working on the case. There are no records now in existence as to what Olson may have found.

Detective Pete Norfleet - Martin Miller, brother to Ben Miller, paid a detective named Pete Norfleet from Hale Center, Texas, to investigate the case. Norfleet paid more than one visit to the Millers while he was investigating. Norfleet sent the Millers a letter saying the gun found in the tree was the gun used in the crime. Norfleet said the matter (murder?) would be settled in a couple of days, but nothing ever happened.

Martin Miller evidently told his children not to tell anyone Norfleet was staying with them. What repercussions did he fear?

CHAPTER 6

THE PEOPLE INVOLVED

Ben Miller

The Sheriff's office brought the clothes Ben had worn the day of the murder to Ola Mae and asked if they were what Ben wore the day he was killed. His family was also asked if they were Ben's clothes. One presumes the Sheriff's Department was trying to establish positive identity of the garments as well as a time line for the killing to show whether Ben had gone home and changed clothes after he dropped off Ola Mae and before he was murdered. The clothes were identified by all parties as the ones worn by Ben that day.

Ola Mae Kimbro

Ola Mae was about 5'5" tall, with an average build. She had blonde hair and blue eyes. She was a quiet girl, not outgoing or putting herself forward. She had six brothers and was the eldest sibling and only girl.

After high school, Ola Mae evidently didn't work except for one short stint in a laundry. She was her mother's pet and wasn't made to do housework or other chores.

She was said to have lain on the bed and read Westerns all day long every day. She and her brother Johnny were both avid readers. Ola Mae would go to the library and get books, one time a whole boxful. Someone asked her if she was going to read all of them. She replied she'd read them within the week and go back for more.

Ola Mae was dating another man before she met Ben. The boyfriend was a ladies man and one whom Ola Mae's brothers warned her against. The man evidently had a bad reputation.

One can imagine a young woman, possibly the favorite child since she was the only girl, who spent all of her time reading romantic Western novels, would have an idealized version in her head of the kind of man, based on the cowboy heroes, she wanted to meet and marry. Was Ben Ola Mae's dream cowboy? Or was the instantaneous attraction one of those larger-than-life events that sometimes happens?

Ola Mae's visit to the Behrensville Rifle Club in Theon with the Georgetown gang may have been a way for her to seek the adventure and romance she probably craved, considering her reading habits. The romantic way in which they met must have been emotionally satisfying to her mind.

Loss Sudduth, leader of the gang, wanted to go with her and was jealous when she left with Ben the night they met. Loss and his gang also didn't like the fact Ben was a German-American from Walburg — possibly another reason for starting a feud. She did tell someone in her later years, she never went anywhere with the Georgetown gang again after that night.

Ola Mae said Ben had twenty-three dollars on his person the night he was murdered. She evidently mentioned to other people Ben usually carried a lot of money on him. Was robbery part of the motive for the killing? Or was the money simply a bonus for the killer(s) who had another motive?

At the time of Ben's death, Ola Mae was twenty-one years old. She and Ben had dated for a year or more before the tragedy and were engaged to be married.

Loss Sudduth

Joseph Losson Sudduth, Jr., aka Loss Sudduth, was born on December 20, 1912. He was almost 18 years old when Ben Miller was killed. He stood about 5'7" tall, and was described as being stocky, or pudgy, with light-colored hair.

Even though no pictures are available of Sudduth, he was described by acquaintances as being of quiet personality. Others felt he could have taken leadership of a gang — that he had it in him to do so.

Sudduth lived in the country near Walburg with his parents, but spent most of his time with friends in North Town. According to the 1929 census information, he dropped out of school after the 7th grade. He had the reputation of not working at a regular job. However, several sources said Sudduth was a gambler and a bootlegger and furnished liquor to the Courthouse and the Sheriff's Department.

Not only was Sudduth a bootlegger, but from other accounts he liked alcohol himself as did most residents in those days. He had a brother who owned a liquor store on Highway 195.

At Christmas and other holidays, Loss drank all day long, then just wanted to sleep. He was considered a good hunter which would have required him to be a good shot.

His gang spent most of their time fighting, gambling, and in other unwholesome pursuits. It is believed Loss was the ringleader of the gang. This would be a bit unusual, since he was only 17 to their age 26, but it is possible.

Since one of the other gang members was his brother-in-law, the family connection may have given him precedence as the leader of the group.

Most of the people interviewed claimed Sudduth was the one who killed Ben Miller, however he was never accused, let alone tried or convicted because of his relationship with local authorities.

Red Williams

Another member of the Georgetown gang was Red Williams. It was difficult to find the correct Williams since there were a number of families in Georgetown with the same last name and several who also had the nickname Red.

The few things known and shared about the Red Williams in the gang was he had married Loss Sudduth's sister and he had a brother named Pete who was mentally challenged (supposedly had the mind of about an 8-year-old).

After much research, it was determined the man who matched these clues was a Finas O. Williams. He was born May 28, 1903 which would have made him 27 years old when the murder occurred.

Red, as he was known, was the youngest child in a very large family. He was big – six feet tall or more and heavy-set. His sandy-colored hair gave him his nickname. One person described him as 'slouchy.' All agree Red was of a mean temperament and a man to be avoided.

Williams married Mamie Lemon Sudduth on November 21, 1920. The 1930 census records show they had a son, Warren. Mamie worked at a dry cleaners. Red never worked, but was a gambler. He also got money from his mother and his wife.

Red ran around on Mamie, but she stayed with him until her death in July of 1946 from pneumonia following a hysterectomy. Five months later on

December 12 of the same year, Red married again, to one Myrtle Leola Parker beside whom he is buried.

Stories told about Red indicated he had quite a temper. One incident came from someone who saw him, while playing a game of dominoes, reach over and grab his partner's glasses and smash them on the table when Red didn't like the domino played.

His reputation was further illustrated by another story which occurred in a small beer joint north of Georgetown. Red evidently loved to fight with a knife and was considered to be a 'mean son-of-a-gun.' He got into a fight with a little guy from Florence just because the little guy had been whipping people. Red was ready to take him on. The smaller man defeated Red, but used a knife to do it.

Burrell Gunn

The third member of the 'gang' was Burrell Gunn. Gunn was also related to the Sudduth family by marriage. Gunn's sister Nettie married Loss's brother Willie Williams Sudduth on November 23, 1928. No descriptions of Gunn are available, although he was partly of American Indian ancestry.

Little is known about Burrell Gunn. Records show he married Lucile Kirkpatrick on October 24, 1931 in Bell County, Texas, a year after the Miller murder. They had one daughter, Patsy Jean. Family stories claim Gunn died of a heart attack while walking upstairs at his parent's house.

Those same accounts describe Gunn as a warm and gentle person who was artistic, good at drawing and chiseling things out of limestone rock such as Indians and other items. Gunn's wife told a relative, however, Gunn was 'like a gypsy." He would evidently be gone for a week, then return home again for a week.

An interesting footnote to this decades old mystery is that supposedly, on his deathbed, Gunn wanted to talk to either Martin Miller or John Miller, Ben's brothers.

For whatever reason, Gunn's family refused to let anyone in to see the dying man, so it was never known what he wanted to tell the Millers. He could, perhaps, have solved the crime had he been allowed to speak.

CHAPTER 7

A PERSON OF INTEREST

The Sheriff panted for breath as he pounded on the door of the Judge's home. He'd hurried to get there even though he knew he wouldn't be a welcome visitor at six o'clock in the morning.

To his surprise, within a few minutes the door opened.

The Judge stood there in shirt and trousers, his paunch overhanging the waistband. His unshaven cheeks revealed a lack of attention to his appearance.

"Lowe. Come in."

Louis Lowe stood still for a moment, taken aback at the abrupt greeting.

Harry Dolan turned and trudged toward the room that served him as an office. Lowe followed close behind. What would have made the judge get up this early in the morning? He knew the man wasn't by nature an early riser.

Lowe knew a grimace twisted one corner of his mouth. Good thing he wasn't facing the judge. Dolan's drinking habits didn't usually make His Honor available until mid-morning most days. So his early rising was unusual to say the least.

Dolan walked into the office, motioned Lowe inside, closed the door, growled a question.

"What is it?"

Lowe ran his fingers over the band of the hat he'd automatically removed when the front door opened.

"There's been a killing."

"I know."

Dolan walked over to his desk, pulled open a bottom drawer, withdrew a bottle and a glass and slammed them on the desk.

He poured himself a drink, gestured toward the bottle and raised his eyebrows in invitation.

Lowe shook his head. One of them needed to have a clear mind. It didn't bode well for the day if the judge started this early.

Dolan slugged back the contents of the glass, stared at Lowe for a moment before he spoke.

"Ben Miller, right?"

"That's right, Judge." He couldn't believe Dolan already knew about the killing. How had the man heard? Lowe had only been awakened and notified a short time before.

"Have you been to the scene?"

"Nope. Sent my deputies. Reckon Faubion and the others are there. Figured you might want to know about it before I went over."

"Unfortunately, I do know about it."

"Because...?"

Dolan poured another drink, swallowed half of it.

"I had an earlier morning visitor."

Lowe stiffened.

"A friend of ours." Dolan swirled the remaining liquid in the glass before he downed it.

"A friend. Did he have something to do with it?"

Dolan's sneer was effective, even with his stubbled cheeks giving him the appearance of a whiskery cherub.

"You could say that."

The judge leaned forward, eyes fixed on the sheriff.

"The crime was committed by a hitchhiker, Lowe. Miller picked up a hitchhiker who killed him for his money, stole his car, and fled the scene."

Dolan's mockery wasn't lost on Lowe.

"But...."

Dolan hit the desk with the empty glass. "No buts, Lowe. Nobody local had anything to do with the crime, got it? It was a hitchhiker."

Lowe stood there, studied the other man. Thoughts raced through the sheriff's mind. Thoughts of supplies of liquor brought into the courthouse at night by friends. Bottles and bottles, a few of which made their way to his department and others to various city and county officeholders. If they didn't want to sever those connections, they'd have to protect their friend.

A sour taste watered his mouth. Too bad about Ben Miller, though. He'd been a decent young man. It wasn't right he shouldn't have real justice done.

"Do we understand each other?"

Dolan's cold tones interrupted his thinking. Lowe

ran his left hand around the rim of his hat, raised his right in a semi-salute.

"Yes, Your Honor."

"Good. Now go away. I have things to do. Let yourself out."

Even before he completed the sentence, Dolan reached for the bottle on his desk.

Lowe turned and walked to the front door. He'd best make an appearance at the crime scene. Wouldn't do to let anyone start speculating about possible killers and maybe figure out the right answer.

The hitchhiker theory needed to be put out now while folk's minds were still in a state of shock. He'd need to be real careful about how he worded the statements that would go to other law enforcement agencies. Didn't want them getting close to the truth.

He hoped this would work. At sixty-one years of age, he didn't need any problems messing up his comfortable life.

****

Harry Dolan

Harry Archible Dolan was born in Taylor, Texas on July 15, 1895. He attended public school in Taylor, Texas, and the University of Texas at Austin where he received his law degree.

Dolan served in the military as a member of the Third Aero Squadron, American Expeditionary Force, during World War I. He held a commission as a lieutenant. He was wounded twice and escaped from No Man's Land after being shot down.

His was an outgoing, boisterous stereotypical Irish personality who reportedly liked his whiskey and women in equal measure. Usually the center of attention in any group where he was found, he was described as squatty, with dark hair. Dolan's official 'judge' picture shows pompadours, a side part, and a self-satisfied expression. Dolan was married and had four children.

Dolan served as Judge of the 26th District Court in Georgetown, Texas, from 1929 – 1942. He came to Georgetown as County Attorney in 1926 and served in that capacity for several years until the office was combined with the office of District Attorney at which time he became District Attorney.

W. H. Nunn was appointed by the governor to fill the unexpired term of deceased Judge Cooper Sansom in 1928, however when Nunn took the bench for the first time, he immediately resigned from the position.

Dolan was nominated by the Williamson County Democratic Executive Committee to serve as judge. At age 33 he was believed to be the youngest nominee in the state for such a position. Dolan was elected and took office on January 1, 1929. He unsuccessfully ran for Congress in 1930 for the 10th Congressional District. Dolan received 3,230 votes, winner J. P. Buchanan 3,302.

Many residents interviewed said Dolan was not a

good person, others plainly said he was a drunk. One individual close to the Dolan family said the Judge didn't have the kind of reputation one would expect or want from a district judge. A source stated that Dolan was known to be so inebriated at times in court that he gave his ruling in a case while lying on the counsel's table.

Several sources related how the judge and others in the courthouse would get drunk and decide to stage a mock trial. They would go to the Ridge, the black area of town — or perhaps have someone in law enforcement go? — grab a black person, drop a handkerchief over their head, and for entertainment bring them to the courthouse where they would try them on some made-up charge.

In 1930, a District Judge had enormous power and could get away with much an ordinary citizen could not.

It was reported from several sources Judge Dolan and Loss Sudduth were drinking buddies even though there was a considerable difference in their ages and situations in life. They were seen a number of times sitting outside drinking at the North Town home where Sudduth visited almost daily. Was Sudduth the source of the alcohol furnished to the courthouse? And was he the reason the Judge didn't want the Sheriff's Department to investigate any local people in the Miller murder? Some have said "yes" to both questions.

An interesting occurrence took place at some point after the murder. It isn't clear from sources reporting as to whether it was weeks or months later, but it may have happened as follows.

****

Walburg, 1930

The door of the small tavern swung open. The bartender raised his eyes, stopped his idle swiping at the bar with a cloth. Two men tried to push past each other to get into the room first.

Obviously guys needing a drink. Or maybe two guys who'd already had way too many drinks.

Two farmers who stood at the other end of the bar also watched as the men made their way across the floor, alternately shoving, then supporting each other.

The taller man poked the other. "Fred, ain't that…?"

Fred looked…looked again. "It's that Judge Dolan from Georgetown. Wonder who he's with?"

The bartender couldn't help but hear their conversation. He would have worried since prohibition was still in effect if he hadn't known the judge's drinking habits. All he could offer today was beer, but he knew it would be fine with His Honor as long as it was alcohol.

He tried to identify Dolan's companion. All of a sudden it registered. Loss Sudduth! An odd pair. Maybe they happened to hit here at the same time, but the fact Dolan's arm was draped across Sudduth's shoulder argued against that theory.

"Afternoon, gents." The bartender straightened as they neared the bar. His experienced eye could tell they were more than the proverbial 'three sheets to the wind.'

"What'll you have?"

Sudduth staggered to the bar and slapped a meaty fist on it. "Beer. Lotsa beer. One for me…." He turned and gave a drunken mock bow toward the man next to him. "And one for my buddy."

The bartender pulled out two bottles, uncapped them, and set them on the bar.

Each man took a long pull, sighed in unison.

A spark of mischief, and sheer curiosity, drew words from the bartender's mouth as he focused on Judge Dolan.

"When did you start runnin' around with Loss Sudduth?"

Dolan threw a drunken arm across Sudduth's pudgy shoulders. "My buddy here? Why I've been running around with him ever since he killed Ben Miller!"

The two drunks nudged each other, smirked, shoved the other's arm a couple of times.

The bartender froze, didn't know where to look. He picked up the rag he'd used to wipe the bar and turned to carefully hang it on a rack behind him.

"Barkeep."

He walked over to the farmers who were nursing their beer.

"Yep?"

"Can you fix us some of that sardine and onion stuff? With the mustard?"

"And lotsa crackers," chimed in the other man.

"Right away."

He focused on placing and delivering their order. He deliberately didn't turn around toward the other patrons until after he heard the final clink of bottles hit the other end of the wooden bar and the sound of the front door being pulled shut.

Only then did he pivot toward the door. Ben Miller...murder!

The men behind him again murmured loud enough for him to hear.

He glanced at them over his shoulder.

"Ya think that Dolan guy was tellin' the truth?" said the taller one.

The other man shrugged, took a swig from his beer bottle. "Dunno. Wouldn't be too healthy for a body to get too curious about somethin' like that, now would it?"

CHAPTER 8

OTHER PEOPLE

Hank Perrizaz

Henry Albert Perrizaz was born January 16, 1899 in Georgetown, Texas. His connection to the Miller murder was through his marriage to Blanche Sudduth, Loss Sudduth's sister and through his apparent ownership of the murder weapon.

Henry, or "Hank" as he was known, was an American citizen whose father had been born in Switzerland. Hank was a rancher.

At the time of the murder, he was 31 years of age. It is not known if he ever participated in the activities of the Georgetown gang, but nothing indicates he did.

Shortly after a gun was found at the Miller murder scene, Perrizaz reported his own gun missing. He said someone must have stolen it out of his car while it was parked on the Georgetown Square over the weekend.

This was the same story Burrell Gunn was reported to have told. Perrizaz, however, is the more likely gun owner.

Since the Miller murder occurred several months or a year earlier — accounts vary - it is odd the report of a missing gun would be connected to the murder unless it was discovered only a short time after the crime.

There is no evidence now available to show Perrizaz played any role in the murder.

Was the gun found at the murder site his gun? There is no way to truly know since all records from the Sheriff's Department have been destroyed.

The theft of the weapon was never reported in the local paper nor was the discovery of the gun.

Edna Zingelmann (Zinglemann)

The girl who dated Ben Miller previous to his meeting Ola Mae Kimbro was a young German-American who lived, as did Ben, in Walburg, Texas, only a few miles from Georgetown.

Edna Zingelmann was several years younger than Ben. A petite five feet tall, she had brown hair and eyes. Even though she often came across as serious and retiring, she had a great sense of humor which she frequently showed. She was one of five sisters.

From all accounts, Ben was her first love.

Ben and Edna, known as Edd, were going steady and one can presume marriage was on at least one mind.

It is not known if Edd was actually present at the

Behrensville Rifle Club in Theon the night Ben met Ola Mae. If so, she was abandoned since Ben took Ola Mae home.

From all accounts, Edd was heartbroken over Ben's death. It must have been difficult for the German girl to see her cherished hopes and dreams come crashing down in such a brutal and unexpected fashion.

The Hitchhiker/Cowboy

Since the Williamson County Sheriff's Department never made an arrest, and since early newspaper reports adamantly insisted no local person was involved in the murder, the unofficial blame fell on a rodeo cowboy who hitchhiked from Georgetown north the morning of the crime.

A rodeo had been held in Georgetown the week prior to the murder in a field across from where Georgetown High School is now. The rodeo was a large one. Reports said a contestant at the rodeo wanted to get a ride to Alvarado, Texas near Fort Worth where a rodeo was being held on the Monday of the murder.

One version of events assumes Ben picked up the cowboy hitchhiker somewhere between Ola Mae's house and the turnoff to his home.

But why would Ben stop for someone on the main highway when he would be turning onto a secondary road in only a few miles? It would have been difficult, if not impossible, for a hitchhiker to flag another ride on a back country road, therefore this theory appears weak.

Some theories say the hitchhiker killed Ben for the car. The driver was supposed to have entered the Alvarado rodeo the next morning (Monday).

A newspaper account says a man fitting the description of the one believed to have done the murder appeared at an unspecified restaurant and ate lunch. Later, it was said, a citizen of the Alvarado community came upon the same man and gave him a lift to Venus, Texas. None of this was ever proved.

The hitchhiker-acting-alone conclusion would also be unlikely. If Miller's car required gas, which it evidently did, the logical thing for the driver to do would have been to stay on the main road, old Highway 81, and get gas in Jarrell or Belton since the car was headed north.

The road leading to Granger was difficult to get to. No one other than a local person would have known how to make the turn before the bridge and proceed into the creek until the road leading to Granger could be accessed.

The service station attendant in Granger reported he heard the driver of the car talking to someone inside the vehicle. If the cowboy was the killer, who would he have been talking to?

Could the killer(s) have been inside the car and paid the cowboy to take the car to Alvarado and abandon it? There was room inside the vehicle to hold one or two other people, especially since the rumble seat had never been installed. Since it was night, the service station attendant probably couldn't see inside, but did hear conversation.

Could the killer(s) have driven the car themselves, been followed by someone in another vehicle, driven to Alvarado and left the Roadster at the side of the highway? That, too, could have been the way it happened.

Years after the murder, Martin Miller, Ben's brother, talked to a Texas Ranger named Fred Olson who later became head of the Rangers in Austin. Olson said he had trailed the cowboy, whose name was Baker, but it is not known what Olson told Miller regarding any findings.

A story in the *Alvarado Bulletin*, dated September 12, 1930, and handwritten notes from a notebook kept by a Georgetown resident revealed some interesting information that could lead to a more accurate account of what involvement Baker may have had.

The newspaper account presents "the car was evidently driven north on Highway No. 2 and was recovered in Alvarado on the road a short distance from the main highway as previously described."

It states Miller's car was found the next morning near Dallas where a farm couple reported seeing a man get out of the car and leave it early that morning as they went to milk their cows. This would strengthen the theory that it was not done by anyone local, for a resident could not have returned to Georgetown before the murder was discovered.

Also, another couple later reported that they had passed through there earlier and someone had tried to jump on their running board.

Further notes mentioned that someone following the horse races was in the Alvarado area because a Mr. Will Edwards was having a horse race at that time. Speculation involved the man following the races wanting to get out of town and trying to get a car to do so. He supposedly killed Miller to get his car

Two different newspaper accounts give conflicting information. One stated the cowboy/hitchhiker wanted to go to Alvarado to be in a rodeo the next day while a second account refers to the horse race and infers that he was going to participate in that. There was never anything factual to clear up the confusion.

The notebook records noted that the writer had heard it was Loss Sudduth who actually committed the murder of Ben Miller.

Based on the information presented before, is the following a possible answer to what really happened?

CHAPTER 9

A COWBOY'S STORY

North Town, 1930

"That was some ride, pardner!"

Baker winced as the pudgy guy slapped for his shoulder, hit his arm instead. Man, this guy was on the way to loaded.

"Thanks."

He turned to walk away.

"Hey, wait a minute. Whyn't you come with me, buddy? Me'n some friends are gonna party. You can be my guest. After all, I just won five bucks on you." His new friend gave him a leer. "Lotsa drink...lotsa girls, whaddya say?"

The cowboy considered, shrugged. He had nothing else to do. He needed to get to Alvarado in the worst way if he was going to enter the rodeo there Monday though. But it was too early to find someone to hitch with. Folks were more leery about giving rides to foot tourists than they used to be. Maybe somebody at this party might have a car and would offer him a ride.

He grinned. Maybe some little fraulein. He'd heard

about the blonde German girls living in the area…saw a few watch him ride earlier. Why not go with this guy?

"You gotta name?"

"Do I got a name? 'Course I got a name. Name's Loss…Loss Sudduth. C'mon. My friends are waitin' over by the car."

Car. The magic word. Now Baker knew he'd stick to this guy like a brother until he could accomplish a ride farther than to a party.

He draped a long arm over the shorter man's shoulders.

"Lead on, friend. Lead on."

The ride through the dark should have been scary, but it went fast. The other two with Sudduth weren't very friendly. In fact, it was the weirdest trio he'd ever seen. They appeared older, too. Forget it. Not his business. He was looking forward to a little fun and relaxation before he hit the highway.

The driver slowed, dropped off the edge of the pavement onto what seemed to be a side road. Ahead and to the right Baker could see the outline of a bridge. They partied on a bridge? Man, how weird.

The car headed downward at a steep angle before it stopped and the doors opened. They all more or less fell out.

"Wait a minnit."

Loss reached under the front seat of the car and Baker heard the clink of glass. "Gotta get the party goin'."

Booze! All right! Maybe this wouldn't be too bad.

The next hour passed with lots of talk and laughter and a continual passing of bottles around the group of young men and women seated on the edges of the bridge. They dangled their feet over the side, not worrying about losing their balance and falling. Dampness rose around them. Baker could almost smell the wetness.

He knew when he'd had enough. He held up his hand the next time the bottle came around and let it pass to the guy next to him. Too bad none of the frauleins acted interested in a cowboy. Oh, well, he really didn't have time for women tonight anyway. He needed to clear his head a bit and try to figure out if he could get the driver...what was his name? Gunn? Get Gunn to give him a ride to Alvarado before morning.

The sound of a motor chugging drifted through the still, cool night air.

"Car comin'."

As if they'd practiced a hundred times, the group hugged the edges of the bridge and watched a Model A Roadster slow to make its careful way along the center of the road.

"Hey, Ben, come join us."

"Ola Mae, we're here. Come have a drink."

The calls, whistles, and waves indicated people the group obviously knew. He could see the couple in the car wave, but the vehicle didn't slow and proceeded on toward town.

Baker became aware of mutterings on his left. A foot or two away, Sudduth threw a bottle into the creek below. It reflected the moonlight peeking from the clouds. The clink and crash of glass echoed through the night air.

"It ain't fair. She shouldn't be going with a dirty German."

Whoa. Sounded as if somebody was more than a little jealous.

Sudduth pushed himself erect, grabbed a railing.

"I'll fix him. I'll fix him good. He ain't gonna get away with this no more."

The younger man swayed. His voice blasted at the others.

"Party's over. Ever-body go home. Shoo." He made a flapping motion like he was herding chickens.

Guffaws and giggles greeted his words and actions.

"I mean it, dammit. Go home. All of you."

Silence fell. No comments were made as the rest of the group slowly got to their feet and moved toward several cars pulled to the side of the road.

Baker noticed only the two pals of Sudduth, Gunn and…what was the other guy's name…Williams? Yeah. They stayed where they were, even though they'd also gotten to their feet.

Sudduth started walking in the direction of the side road where Gunn had parked the car.

The cowboy stood erect, stretched. What should he do?

"Hey, pard." He pitched his voice loud enough for Sudduth to hear. "Can you guys give me a ride for a ways north? I need to make a rodeo tomorrow in

Alvarado."

The three wheeled and stared at him. The moon was bright enough he could make out the expressions on their faces without any problem.

Williams and Gunn wore matching scowls.

Sudduth's face initially reflected irritation, too, until a series of unidentifiable emotions ended in a look of unholy glee. He slid his hand inside his pants pocket, back out again, a satisfied look on his face.

"Yeah, sure. We can work out somethin'. Come on, cowboy. Let's get to the car and we'll talk about it."

Baker trailed the three, watched as Williams and Gunn caught up to Sudduth. The trio started an animated conversation. He heard a protest from Gunn, saw a shrug by Williams. Sudduth patted his pocket, leaned toward them and dropped his voice even lower.

A shiver snaked its way down the cowboy's spine. What were these three hatching? Was he in some kind of danger from them? He'd better be watchful. He might be wearing boots, but he could move fast if he needed to.

He continued to trail behind, alert for whatever came next.

When they reached the car, Sudduth gestured to Gunn who slid behind the wheel of the vehicle and started the engine. It coughed a couple times before it caught.

Baker started to hurry, then realized they weren't leaving. Gunn pulled onto a track evidently serving as the road, backed the car until it sat square in the middle, effectively blocking the way.

The cowboy caught up to the others.

Gunn turned off the engine and got out of the car.

"Aren't we leaving?" Baker tried not to let apprehension tint his words.

"In a while. In a while." Sudduth sounded loud in the quiet of the night.

The combination of an occasional call of a night bird, the gentle gurgle of the shallow creek, and the smell of rotted vegetation made the hair on Baker's neck stand on end.

He took a deep breath and schooled himself to patience.

Felt like forever, but it could only have been fifteen or twenty minutes later when the sound of a car motor could be heard coming from town.

"Do what I said." Sudduth's low order to Gunn and Williams shattered the calm of the night.

Baker watched as the two got into the car and started the engine. At the end of the pathway, they veered right and disappeared under the bridge. The motor noise cut off.

The younger man turned toward Baker. He walked toward the cowboy, gave him another of the irritating slaps on the arm.

"We're gonna play a little trick on a friend of ours and you can help. We'll let you borrow his car and drive it to Alvarado so you can git to your rodeo."

Baker tried to comprehend. "What do I do with the car when I get there?"

"Leave it by the side of the road when you hit town. We'll come get it tomorrow and you won't have to worry about it."

Baker thought for a moment, shrugged. "Sounds good to me."

"Fine, fine. You get over here next to Red. Burrell's gonna pretend to be almost passed out. You can support him on his other side. When the guy drivin' stops, you follow Red's lead. I'm gonna surprise him from the side." He snickered a drunken giggle.

Nerves tightening, the cowboy thought briefly about leaving this bunch and heading out on his own. Only problem was, in the dark, it would be hard to find his way out of this place and get safely headed in the right direction. He didn't want to end up in the middle of the creek at night...especially since he had no idea how deep the water was.

No, he'd have to play out this childish prank and get the car and directions before he could leave these guys behind.

"Get ready." Sudduth's order came from the right as he melted into some bushes next to the track.

Baker moved slowly next to Gunn and put his arm around him. Alcohol fumes from the men caused a wave of nausea before he steadied himself.

The car motor sounded louder.

Now he could tell the car had braked and slowed to make the left turn off the road. Must be a short cut the locals used.

Headlights blinded him as the other car skidded to

a stop a few feet from where he and the others stood.

"Hey."

He heard Williams' voice ring out.

No response from the car.

"Give us a hand."

Williams moved forward, half-dragging Gunn. Red shot a glare at the cowboy.

Baker realized it was his cue to help the limp Gunn along.

He and Williams half-dragged, half-carried Gunn. When they reached the front end of the stopped vehicle, Williams repeated his demand.

"Give us a hand with Gunn."

Baker saw a match flare inside the car. Must be lighting up.

A loud report ripped the night silence.

The cowboy dropped his arm from Gunn's shoulders.

Baker startled. "What's going on?"

A second sharp sound penetrated the nocturnal hush.

Baker took a couple of steps forward. Once out of the glare in his eyes, his vision quickly adjusted to the dark surrounding them.

Loss Sudduth stood at the passenger side of the car. By the moonlight, the cowboy could see the half smirk twisting the man's mouth.

He also saw the figure of a man slumped forward over the steering wheel. Leaping forward, Baker grabbed Sudduth's shoulder, shook it with force.

"What did you do?"

Sudduth pulled back. "He never should have gone with her. She was supposed to be mine."

Baker tore his hat from his head and threw it on the ground. Flabbergasted didn't begin to describe his emotions.

"You shot a man. Twice. Are you crazy?"

He held out his hand. "Give me the gun."

Sudduth came out of what had been a semi-trance. "Nope. It's borrowed and I need to give it back."

The two of them struggled for possession of the weapon. Sudduth was stronger than he appeared. Maybe there were a few muscles beneath all the flab.

Suddenly, the weapon was ripped from their grasping hands.

Red Williams flung the gun up and over his head.

Baker couldn't tell where it landed. An urgent need to get away swept over him.

"You can't kill a man for no reason. We've gotta get a doctor...or the sheriff."

Sudduth snickered. "Don't bother. One can't help him and the other one won't."

The cowboy didn't understand the cryptic comment, knew he needed to drop what must be a nasty local matter, and get on his way.

"Y'all do what you need to do, but I've gotta get going." He eased away from the trio.

Sudduth glared at him. "We had a deal. You helped me, now I'll help you. Let's get that piece of trash out of the car and you can get on your way."

Baker stopped and thought. Fine. No skin off his

nose. If they wanted to kill each other in this one-horse town, so be it. He'd be far away before anyone ever knew what happened. He didn't intend to stick around to tell. These guys could handle their own lives…he had a rodeo to get to.

Williams and Sudduth moved toward the victim's car, opened the driver's door, reached in and tugged at the lifeless man inside. They pulled until the body slid out the door and landed in the road.

Sudduth leaned over, checked the dead man's pockets, pulled out a roll of bills. He took his foot and pushed the body onto its back, shoved, and watched it roll part way down the embankment next to the track. He leaned forward and pawed at something on the floor of the vehicle.

Baker saw a slim white cylinder drop out of the car and get kicked off the gravel path toward where the body lay.

The guy's cigarette.

Gunn stayed by the car, noisily being sick.

The stench of his vomit tainted the cool early morning air.

"Let's go," ordered Sudduth. "Burrell, pull over and let us get by. We'll lead the way. You got gas?"

Gunn wiped his mouth with a shaky hand, nodded affirmation.

"Cowboy, you drive this car. I'll ride with you. Red, you go with Burrell."

Baker climbed into the roadster and started the engine, checked the gauges on the dashboard. "It's almost outta gas."

"No problem." Sudduth slid into the passenger's side. "We know a place. Pull around Gunn's car and do what I tell you."

Ten minutes later, they'd made the tight half turn under the bridge and headed along the creek bank. A couple of hundred yards later, the cowboy was directed to enter the creek and drive. A short time later, the faint outline of a road appeared on the left. Sudduth gestured him onto the road and they forged ahead. Gunn's car followed closely.

A short time later, Baker could make out the outline of a building on what appeared to be the outskirts of a small town. One dim bulb burned by a lone gas pump.

"Over there. He's open all night. Stop here. Let me get in back. I don't want to be seen."

"Open at this time of the morning? That's crazy."

The younger man snickered. "You'd be surprised how many customers he has during the night. You might say he has a little side business going. A liquid one. He's always open."

Sudduth handed Baker some money. "Get as much gas as you can for this. It should be enough to get you away. Ask the guy how to get to Hearne...it'll help throw anybody off track if they question him."

Baker nodded, waited while Sudduth climbed into the back in the space where a rumble seat would go. The car shook as the younger man squirmed around trying to get out of sight.

A muffled oath spoke of the trouble he was having.

"Okay." Sudduth's voice sounded hollow from the

back. "Get the gas and don't get chatty."

"Right."

Baker pulled up to the lone gas tank, stopped the car, opened the door and waited for someone to appear.

Sudduth's voice again sounded. "Remember, keep it short."

The cowboy didn't respond as a man appeared in the doorway of the building. The gas station attendant stretched and yawned.

"'Mornin'. Whatcha need?"

Baker checked the cash he clutched in his fist. "Uh, gimme a coupla bucks worth of gas."

The man nodded without further talk, walked over to the gas tank, inserted the hose and filled the car with the requested amount.

"That'll be two bucks." He held out his hand.

Baker pulled the cash from his own fist, realized it was a ten he held.

"I'll need change."

The man nodded. "Be right back." He headed inside the building.

"Hurry up," Sudduth hissed. "I'm feelin' like a rag doll full of stuffing crammed in here."

"He went to get change." Baker kept his voice low. "He should be right back. Yep. Here he comes."

"Stop talkin'." Sudduth warning was succeeded by the sound of the attendant's footsteps on the concrete apron.

"Here you are, mister. Eight bucks."

"Thanks." The cowboy stuffed the bills in his

pocket, climbed in the car and brought the engine to life, then remembered.

"Is this the road to Hearne?"

"Yup. Follow until you see the sign where to turn."

"Right. Thanks."

Baker eased out the clutch, gave it some gas, and pulled away from the station.

In the rearview mirror, Baker saw the man watch them for a moment. He saw the guy shrug, head inside.

"Is he out of sight?"

Sudduth's question startled him. For a minute, he'd forgotten his passenger.

"Yep."

"Good. Pull over to the side of the road as soon as the station is out of sight and stop. We'll wait for the others."

The cowboy did as directed, let the motor idle while they waited in silence.

A few minutes later headlights swept up from behind. The oncoming vehicle came to a stop at their bumper.

"Help me outta here." Sudduth struggled to free himself from his cramped position.

Baker tugged until the younger man was free and standing on the road.

They walked to where Gunn's car idled.

"Burrell, I'm gonna ride with you and Red now." Sudduth turned toward Baker. "Mister, I'm gonna let you have this car. We'll drive in front of you and take you to the highway where you can head on to

Alvarado. When you get there, dump the car along the road before you hit town. We'll pick it up later."

Baker nodded. "Right." Some imp of mischief made him doff his Stetson to the ungodly trio. "Nice doin' business with you gents."

He turned, entered the dead man's car, waited for the others to lead the way.

What a crazy night. A man dead, a car stolen. But now he had money in his pocket and the doin's in Alvarado were calling him.

Be weird if he won the purse at the rodeo. If he didn't at least he still had a stake to go on until he could win something…or maybe he should steal something. He patted his pocket.

Seemed to work for these guys.

CHAPTER 10

WHATEVER HAPPENED TO. . .

Ben Miller —

Funeral services for Ben were held, beginning at the home of his brother Martin, near the Berry Creek schoolhouse. They were concluded at the Lutheran cemetery where interment was made beside his parents.

Services were conducted by Rev. J. R. Sieck, pastor of the Lutheran church in Walburg where Miller was a member. Funeral arrangements were in charge of the Davis Undertaking Department. A description of the funeral service was detailed in a local newspaper article.

The funeral was reported to have been attended by a large number of relatives and friends.

Ben's car was returned to his brother Martin who later sold it to a Fred Widmer. Widmer kept the Model A until his wife left one day in the car and was never seen again.

Ola Mae Kimbro —

Ola Mae had been taking instruction to become a member of Ben's church so they could be married there. On April 5, 1931, Ola Mae Kimbro was confirmed as an adult in the Zion Lutheran Church. Her confirmation verse was I Corinthians 6:20 – "For ye are bought with a price: therefore glorify God in your body, and in your spirit, which are God's."

A couple of years later, Ola Mae married Willard Fletcher on March 4, 1933. Four children resulted from the union.

Her husband died in 1957 leaving Ola Mae with a ten-year-old daughter to rear on her own. Ola Mae worked as a "lunchroom lady" at a local elementary school until she retired.

She died on August 30, 2006, in Georgetown, only two days before her 97th birthday.

Loss Sudduth —

Sudduth married Cleo Irene Montgomery, a North Town resident, on December 26, 1939, nine years after Ben Miller was killed and six years after Ola Mae Kimbro married. Loss and Cleo had gone together for years. They had no children and lived on the corner of Morrow Street & Austin Avenue, now the location of a Papa John's Pizza.

Did he hope during those years before Ola Mae married she might turn to him? He had desperately wanted to go with her. Or did she suspect some connection with Ben's death and avoid Loss?

Sudduth never worked at a regular job by all accounts in his younger years but let his wife support him.

When it became necessary to move a cemetery from the Mexican border in order to build Falcon Dam in the early '50s, the contractor who would handle the removal, one Sidney Perrin, came to Georgetown trying to find someone to dig and move the graves. He hired Loss Sudduth. After this job was completed, through the experience gained, Sudduth reportedly became one of the best backhoe operators in the area.

Sudduth died on November 22, 1985 at the age of 72 of a heart attack. He is buried in Berry's Creek Cemetery near Georgetown.

It is ironic Sudduth died on November 22nd – the same month and day as the month and day Ben Miller was born.

Red Williams –

It isn't known what profession, if any, Williams ever had. He died November 11, 1981 in Brackenridge Hospital in Austin. He was 78 years old. He is buried at the Odd Fellows Cemetery with a joint headstone with his second wife Myrtle, who passed away in 1993.

Burrell Gunn —

Gunn died young at the age of 27, four years after the Miller murder.

The doctor's certificate showed Gunn died of aortic regurgitation and that medical attention had been given him for a little over a month before death occurred. Family members and descendants, however, reported he had a heart attack while walking upstairs at his parents' house.

He left a wife and daughter.

Harry Dolan —

Dolan died at the age of 46 on December 18, 1942 from gastric hemorrhage (a medical term usually associated with the results of long-term drinking).

In the obituary for Harry Dolan, after all the flowery praise common to such articles in those days, follows a list of pallbearers, many well-known and/or distinguished individuals. Last pallbearer's name on the list? Loss Sudduth.

Edna Zingelmann (Zinglemann) —

Edd married Roy Lee Headrick in 1933, three years after Ben's death. Their son, Roy Lee, Jr., was born in 1934. They had four children in all.

Edna died March 18, 1973 at the age of 62.

Louis Lowe —

Lowe died on September 15, 1955, at the age of 86 according to the death certificate, probably of heart failure due to a long standing heart condition.

Hank Perrizaz —

Perrizaz died on July 29, 1968 at Brackenridge Hospital in Austin, Texas at the age of 69.

The Cowboy/Hitchhiker —

Baker died in prison for killing a truck driver.

CHAPTER 11

IN THE END

It is clear the investigation of the Ben Miller murder case was not handled with normally accepted police procedures. Statements are not usually given to the press immediately after a crime is committed saying "no one local had anything to do with it."

There is no record any local witnesses were even interviewed — indeed the only person the law apparently talked to was the man (or men) who discovered the body. Why would the officers not interview everyone even remotely connected to the case to look for clues?

Is it really believable the Sheriff's Department was unaware of the 'feud' between the gang and Ben Miller? Did they not know the gang existed? Or had they been told to ignore the gang's activities considering who the leader was?

Why did it take so long after the murder for the gun to be found? Was the area never searched by authorities? Why this wasn't done at the time of the initial investigation can be ascribed either to sloppy procedure by the Department or to a cover-up.

It is also strange that no newspaper account exists of the discovery of the gun. Everything else about the murder was printed. Why would this important piece of evidence never be publicized? Again...sloppy reporting...or cover up?

There had been a huge rainstorm the Wednesday preceding the murder. A storm heavy enough the opening of a County Fair was postponed one day due to the weather. Wouldn't the soil, especially in the area of a creek, have been moist enough for footprints to be found? Or the tire tracks of the second car? Or were they ignored if they were there?

Ben had twenty-three dollars in his pocket. It was a fair sum of money during Depression days. Yet his killer(s) spent money to buy gas in Granger. Ben's money? Most young men probably carried all the money they had on their persons in those days since the country was recovering its financial health and banks were considered unreliable.

Ben may also have given the impression he had more money than he did since he drove a new car and dressed in suits. Ola Mae also frequently told people how well off Ben was financially.

After the murder weapon was found, only then did Hank Perrizaz report that a gun had been previously stolen out of his car. Why would he not have reported it sooner if it was indeed stolen? Was he providing an alibi for someone who might have 'borrowed' his gun? Or was the weapon truly stolen by someone who knew that Perrizaz had the gun and where he kept it?

The killer(s) had to be familiar with the local geography to take the route used from Georgetown to Granger or, as has been fictionalized, a local had to direct the driver. A newspaper report at the time states it was believed after securing the car and throwing Miller's body halfway down the embankment, the car was driven over the ground Miller intended to take.

The car passed under the bridge and took a cross-country road by Weir to Granger where it intersected Highway 2-B. There, the newspaper continued, the killer(s) inquired about the road leading to Hearne.

Instead of taking the Hearne road, the car continued north on the highway through Temple, Waco, and on to Alvarado, near Fort Worth, where the vehicle was abandoned. The newspaper further reported "That he [the driver] was driving fast is indicated by the fact a mailbox on the road toward Weir from the bridge had been run over and the post on which it was placed pulled up bodily. The car is said to have backed away from the post and continued."

As mentioned earlier, there was evidently a party of boys and girls on the Dry Berry Creek Bridge the night of the murder. The group supposedly stopped a local doctor from Walburg, a Dr. Wiedemeyer, when he drove over the bridge returning to Walburg. He had a Model A Ford the same color and style as Ben's. When it was seen the driver wasn't Ben, the group sent him on his way.

If this actually happened, and after the murder was discovered, why would the doctor not have reported the incident to the law? It would be a reasonable conclusion for an intelligent man to make that somehow one or more of the group of young people might have been involved in the crime or knew something about it.

Or did the doctor tell the Sheriff's Department and his story was ignored or suppressed?

Why did none of the young people put two and two together and report their presence at the scene earlier in the evening? Were they perhaps afraid of retribution at the hands of some local person(s) involved in the slaying? Or were they protecting themselves from the illegal drinking they had done?

Besides being 'drinking buddies,' reports were Dolan and Sudduth were also hunting companions. One report said Dolan was a good friend of one of the North Town families. An aunt in that family named several of the kinfolk's children and she gave one the middle name Dolan.

Many questions have been raised about the crime, especially as research into the case has taken place. Perhaps upon publication of this book, other information may yet surface.

Hopefully a desire for the truth will replace fear for those who might know more.

AUTHOR'S NOTE

It has been an interesting journey investigating and writing about the murder of Ben Miller. Eighty-four years is a long time for the death of someone to go unsolved. Many of the Miller family, of course, have passed on, but the concept of wanting justice for someone slain still exists in the minds and hearts of others connected to the characters or the case. My hope is this book may help bring some kind of closure for them.

With all the ingredients present in the story, it was a natural for a thrilling fiction tale. I chose to write it as a non-fiction book and have tried to be true to the information available though so many official records are missing. Hopefully it has been presented in a readable fashion.

In today's twenty-first century, police procedural investigations have progressed to higher levels than ever before. If modern investigative techniques had been applied to the case, no doubt there would have been an arrest and a conviction in the murder. The chances of a 'cover-up' are probably less likely today than ever before given our electronic world and the easy transmission/sharing of information through various media. The newspaper industry has come a long way as well. Modern-day reporters are pretty good investigators themselves and have helped in the solution of many a crime.

If the case were investigated today, any number of people connected to Ben Miller would have been interviewed. And there is the possibility any one of them did commit the murder. But when all of the available evidence was studied, circumstantial though it is, only one name continued to surface as the person guilty of killing Ben Miller, and it is the conclusion presented in this book.

Bottom line?

Only God truly knows who the murderer was and He will mete out His justice for the crime at the appropriate time.

ADDENDUM

MORE LOCAL HISTORY

WILLIAMSON COUNTY

Originally the area now known as Williamson County was part of Milam County. The Anglo settlement began during the Texas Revolution.

At the time, Indian attacks were common. To help solve the problem a military post was built near the headwaters of Brushy Creek (now southwestern Williamson County).

Named for Capt. John J. Tumlinson, Jr., the post held a company of Texas Rangers whose mission was to defend the area from the Indians. It was active until February, 1836, when it was abandoned to let the Rangers help deal with the Mexican invasion of Texas.

In 1838 the first civilian settlement was established by a Dr. Thomas Kenney and a party of settlers. They built a fort (Kenney's Fort) on Brushy Creek, near the site of the current crossing of the MKT Railroad (known as the Katy Railroad).

Other sites on Brushy Creek were established soon after, but Indian raids still kept pioneer settlement in check. Many settlers, including Kenney, were killed by Indians in succeeding years.

By 1842 many of the early farms were abandoned when Governor Sam Houston advised settlers to pull back from what was then the frontier.

After 1846, the Indian threat was reduced and part of those settlers who had come to Texas after its annexation into the U.S., traveled to the Brushy Creek area and the San Gabriel River. By 1848 there were at least 250 settlers in part of Milam County. In the early months of the year a petition was signed by almost half of them to organize a new county.

The Texas Legislature realized the settlers in the area needed a closer seat of government than the one for Milam County, so they established Williamson County on March 13, 1848.

The county was originally to have been named San Gabriel County, but was instead named after Robert McAlpin Williamson (aka Three-Legged Willie), a Texas statesman and judge.

The county seat, Georgetown, was laid out during the summer and a district court was in session by October.

At one point during the Depression years Federal agents reportedly came in and killed a bunch of cattle to keep from having an oversupply of beef. This was supposed to get the economy jump-started by limiting availability of the meat, thereby raising prices. They reportedly paid the owners between $1.35 - $1.50 a head. The agents shot the animals and put them in a ditch, supposedly wouldn't give them to the people to eat.

All the deer and armadillos were killed out in Williamson County during the Depression. The armadillos were often called "Hoover Hogs." Calling armadillos Hoover hogs was only one way in which President Herbert Hoover's name was used to state citizen dissatisfaction with the Great Depression. Temporary encampments for homeless individuals were called Hoovervilles. Newspapers used by people sleeping outdoors were called Hoover blankets. The term Hoover hog was also used to refer to rabbits and jackrabbits hunted and eaten. However, the name stuck to the armadillo over the long term.

(Some information excerpted from: Mark Odintz, "WILLIAMSON COUNTY," Handbook of Texas Online. Published by the Texas State Historical Association.)

GEORGETOWN, TEXAS

Georgetown was named for George Washington Glasscock who donated the land for the town. Early

American and Swedish pioneers were attracted to the area's abundance of timber and good, clear water. In addition, the land was extremely fertile and inexpensive.

The city is the county seat of Williamson County. Southwestern University, the oldest university in Texas, was founded in 1840 and is located about one-half mile from Georgetown's historic town square. Sun City Texas is a large retirement community that constitutes more than one-third of Georgetown's population.

The North and Middle Forks of the San Gabriel River both run through the city, providing over 30 miles of hike and bike trails, several parks and recreation for residents and visitors alike.

North Town, the home of many of the people involved in this story, was annexed by ordinance on May 10, 1954 by the City of Georgetown.

Georgetown was dry for many years until voters began to approve various ordinances to allow alcohol sales. Whether an area of town was wet or dry was controlled mostly by local political subdivisions in the city.

The issue became more confusing since some areas opted for mixed beverages only, others beer and wine only, others a combination of all. The last of the ordinances passed in recent years took place in 2010. There are still a couple of commercial addresses in Georgetown that are dry.

Without question the single most important issue relating to economic development was the location of Interstate 35 through Georgetown. Originally, when first conceived, a Georgetown route was very much in doubt as most alignments had the road going through or near Taylor, Texas.

Round Rock and Georgetown leadership strongly lobbied for a route along the Balcones Escarpment fault line, a line which would later become the U.S. Highway 81 mentioned in this book, and later, Interstate 35.

Georgetown was an agrarian community for most of the 19th and early 20th centuries. The Shawnee Trail, a cattle trail leading from Texas to the rail centers in Kansas and Missouri, crossed through the heart of Georgetown. Current Williams Drive was then the Andice Road. Old State Highway 81 is where Austin Avenue is now. There are still some old street signs in Georgetown that read State Highway 81.

The establishment of Southwestern University in 1873 and construction of a railroad in 1878 contributed to the town's growth and importance. A stable economy developed, based largely on agricultural activity. Cotton was the dominant crop in the area between the 1880s and the 1920s. Williamson County was the top producer of cotton in the State of Texas.

Population growth and industrial expansion continued modestly in the twentieth century until about 1960 when residential, commercial, and industrial development, due to major growth and urban expansion of nearby Austin, greatly accelerated. Georgetown's population was 47,400 at the 2010 census.

In 2008, Fortune Small Business Magazine named Georgetown the No. 2 best city in the nation to "live and launch" a new business. Its historic downtown square is marketed as the "Most Beautiful Town Square in Texas."

WALBURG, TEXAS

Walburg was originally known Possum Creek, then for a short time as Concordia. It is an unincorporated German farming community located on Farm Road 972, about 11.5 miles northeast of the city of Georgetown. It started with 16 people in 1890 and with a few ups and downs has remained at about 250, estimated in 1990.

A man named Henry Doering moved to the area in 1881 and opened a general store a year later. In 1886 he added a post office, and at that time renamed the town Walburg after his hometown of Walburg, Germany.

In 2000 there was still a population of 250 with eight businesses. Two well-known restaurants are active in the area today and draw customers from throughout the state, particularly on weekends for live music.

Two Lutheran churches (Zion Lutheran, 1882, St. Peter's, 1889) were established. Both are still active today. Zion Lutheran (the newer) is on top of a hill; St. Peter's (the older church) is below. There are two cemeteries, each maintained by one of the churches.

The two World Wars had a severe impact on Zion Lutheran Church's activities in Walburg. The two Lutheran churches and the Catholic church conducted services in German.

The families who lived there didn't want their young people going with the Georgetown Americans because if they married, they wouldn't have been able to go to the Lutheran church unless the American converted. One way around this was if the unconverted spouse 'promised' to convert. Then they could attend church.

The church has in more modern times, changed its policies on marriage to be inclusive to other faiths.

The people of Walburg didn't like Ben Miller, one of their own, going to Georgetown to pick up Ola Mae due to the conflict between the German-American and American communities. The Walburg residents didn't want the Georgetown young people participating in the same events or getting to know each other for fear the young people would marry.

During World War I, a wave of ultra-patriotic feeling swept the country and suddenly people speaking German were labeled as anti-American.

Many sister Lutheran congregations in Texas were mistreated or had paint daubed on their churches. Walburg didn't experience such severe problems, but they immediately did add an English service to their church.

In World War II, German-spoken services were stopped entirely.

The schools also experienced changes. In 1916 the German language spoken in public schools in Walburg and other German communities was dropped due to circumstances created by World War I and the pressures put on the German-speaking people by other Americans.

Today, Walburg is a small, but interesting slice, of Texas history with several original buildings still in existence. The food and music? Well worth a day trip to the area.

ങ

Death of a Juror

D. A. FEATHERLING

ACKNOWLEDGMENTS

Thanks to William Henry Schkade, Jr.
for beginning the investigation
~ and ~
Weldon Mersiovsky
for bringing it to my attention.

Special thanks to the many people in the
Georgetown, Texas civic and judicial departments
who cheerfully provided research assistance and to
private individuals who provided useful information.

CHAPTER 1

26th Judicial Court, Georgetown, Texas
February 6, 1931

"We intend to prove, Gentlemen of the Jury, that Will Edmondson brutally and with malice aforethought murdered Fred Bolinger, his supposed best friend, in cold blood over a matter of mere acres. Land of small importance when weighed against the value of a human life."

The Prosecuting Attorney made a dramatic gesture toward the defendant, accompanied by a sneer. He held the pose for a moment before he turned to the lead Defense Attorney and gave a slight bow.

"Counselor."

~ ~ ~

Thus may have begun the opening statement of the trial that attempted to convict a man of murder for the fifth time...a trial that later ended the life of another man.

Will Edmondson, San Saba County rancher and

farmer, was charged by indictment with the murder of his neighbor, Fred Bolinger, a forty-two year old bachelor. Bolinger was shot at home on the morning of November 10, 1925.

Edmondson was tried four previous times for the murder, but no jury had convicted him. The case was tried twice in San Saba County, where it originated, before being transferred to Llano and heard twice, and then to Williamson County.

In previous trials, Edmondson received a life sentence and 15 years imprisonment at his first two trials. When the case was sent to Llano County on a change of venue, he received 99 years. The court of criminal appeals reversed that decision and a fourth trial ended in a hung jury. The fifth trial would end when a juror became ill.

The change of venue from Llano County to Williamson County brought the case to the 26th District Court where it originally was to be tried on Monday, December 28th, 1930.

For whatever reasons, the trial did not begin until Monday, February 8, Judge Harry Dolan presiding. The regular jury list of forty-eight men and a special venire of one hundred men were the base from which a jury of twelve was finally empaneled.

Walter Leschber gave a discreet swipe at his brow. Why was he sweating so? Of course, it wasn't every day he was called to be a juror, especially in such a high-profile case. He was a farmer and wasn't exactly eager about the experience of serving. On the other hand, it made a change from his ordinary routine.

He'd certainly have something to talk about at the next family gathering, or at church, after the trial was done.

A small wave of excitement swept over him. Perhaps it wouldn't be too bad. It might even be interesting.

He studied the bank of lawyers brought in by the two sides. Smart, well-dressed...exactly how he'd pictured city lawyers. Clever, educated men. Men after the truth? Or simply ones trying to make money out of someone else's misery?

A close look at the defendant didn't help him assess the man. Couldn't tell much about somebody who kept his head down and whispered to an attorney all the time. How would the jury ever know for sure if he was guilty? They'd tried Edmondson four times already and now they'd moved the trial again out of the area where the crime was committed.

He would try his best to listen and determine what the truth was. A tug at his Sunday shirt collar relieved a bit of pressure at his throat...a swallow the dryness of his mouth. His physical discomfort made him wonder if he'd taken his medication that morning. Yes. Now he remembered. He had, and should be all right. He leaned forward and directed his full attention to the courtroom.

The defense and prosecution were each represented by an array of legal talent. The prosecuting State legal team consisted of District Attorney D. B. Wood of Georgetown, O. A. Walton, San Saba and T. H. Hammond, District Attorney 32nd District, Burnet. The defense was represented by Attorney J. F. Taulbee, Georgetown, James H. Baker, San Saba, and Callaway and Darrow of Brownwood, Texas.

Shortly after noon the jury selection began. The first juror chosen was Otto Hartman of Thrall. The other jurors were: G. A. Logan, Georgetown; J. B. Goode, Jarrell; Walter Leschber, Thrall; J. B. Smart, Florence; F. B. Ritchey, Beaukiss; J. W. Green, Florence; O. B. Downing, Hutto; F. E. Buchholz, Georgetown; Sterling Frymire, Jarrell; Edgar Vaught, Georgetown, and Otto Miller, Jarrell.

Each of the jurors was asked "Have you any conscientious scruples against the infliction of death as a punishment for crime, in the proper cases and when prescribed by law?" This seemed to indicate how the state intended to pursue prosecution.

The twelve chosen obviously indicated they had no such problem or they wouldn't have been allowed to serve. An entire list of the jurors on the special venire showed a large number who did have such an objection, so perhaps it was a challenge to find twelve who could serve.

Other questions to the potential jurors indicated

the State would rely on a chain of circumstantial evidence regarding the crime since it would be supported by the testimony of an alleged accomplice.

Will Edmondson was about to be tried…again.

CHAPTER 2

The crime was noteworthy because of the reputation and stature of the defendant Will Edmondson. Edmondson was a wealthy cattleman and farmer who lived in the northeast portion of San Saba County. He was charged by indictment with murder in connection with the death of a neighbor, Fred Bolinger.

The case promised sensation and drama which caused large crowds to attend the trial. Witnesses were so numerous they thronged the rotunda of the Courthouse.

The first witness introduced by the State was Eb Shaw, a seventy-year-old friend and neighbor of the victim. Shaw testified he had visited Bolinger on the morning of November 10th, and, getting no answer, walked into the dimly-lighted two-room house.

Inside he found Bolinger alive on the bed, a bullet wound in his left breast. A few minutes later, another neighbor, Jeems Jones, came in having made arrangements with Shaw and Bolinger to go to town, and found a small caliber pistol lying on a pair of overalls on the floor.

Jones picked up the pistol and took it to one of the only two doors in the house and held it to the light to examine it.

Walter couldn't believe his ears. They found the old man still alive? Why didn't they call the sheriff? Or some law enforcement person? Did they call a doctor? If Bolinger was alive, how was it murder?

He studied the defendant, Edmondson, again. Had he really killed the man? Someone supposedly his friend? How could he have done that? This was better than a picture show. His excitement mounted.

Woods cross-examined by asking Shaw if he killed Fred Bolinger. Shaw's vehement response was he did not, that Bolinger was among his best friends. Shaw's testimony lasted more than three hours.

Walter gave a surreptitious stretch. His shoulders and neck radiated stiffness and a bit of pain. He wasn't used to sitting for hours on end, listening to other people talk. He thought of the fields he usually tended, the small house where his family lived, Dora and the children. A small smile twitched at one corner of his mouth. A soon-to-be new addition to the family would give one more child to love. He'd rather be out plowing a field than sitting here in his Sunday best listening to what men could do to each other. His earlier excitement had waned. It was getting boring. He flexed his shoulders again. Surely they would be through soon. He hoped so. His brain was beginning to fuzz and that was never a good thing.

Testimony by other witnesses established Bolinger always had money, he loaned it to his friends in need, and he had a lot of cash on him at the time of his death. Jeems Jones, Bolinger's friend, further testified the size of the wad of cash was about as big as his arm and consisted of bills, with nothing less in it than fives and tens. Accounts of the trial don't reveal who discovered the cash after the murder or where it was stashed.

Further questioning of Jones provided a disparity of answers to questions he had been asked in previous trials. He testified he reached Bolinger's home about eight o'clock on Monday morning and found Shaw there, saw Bolinger wounded, the bullet hole in his clothing, but saw no bullet hole in the bed clothes or powder burns on the victim or bed.

Previous testimony had established there were only two doors and no windows in the house so lighting was dim at best.

Jones stated he picked up the pistol from the floor and found two shells in it. He examined the pistol at the door in the dim light flickering through the opening.

During his testimony, discrepancies again

surfaced from Jones' previous statements in the other Edmondson trials. Jones said the wounded Bolinger stated he had shot a hole in the roof when he let his pistol go off accidentally.

A Dr. O. D. Nelson testified as to the wound and Bolinger's condition when the doctor arrived at Bolinger's home and sent him to the hospital in Brownwood.

Dr. F. M. Burk of Brownwood testified concerning Bolinger's wound, of the victim's time in the hospital and Bolinger's ultimate death. Bolinger had developed gangrene and pneumonia which ultimately killed him. At that point, the case became a murder.

Hospitals. He hated hospitals. He felt his body cringe at the thought of being confined to a small room containing only a bed and maybe a table day after day. No wonder the old guy hadn't lived. Who would in such circumstances?

It was odd about the guy shooting a bullet hole in his own roof. If he did. Of course, he understood how it could happen. If a man wasn't careful...or if he tended to be jumpy...and a gun was present...all kinds of weird things could happen.

That was one reason he didn't keep guns around the house. He figured he would be pretty safe if he owned one, but you never knew.

He returned his attention to the witness box.

Other witnesses included a carpenter who examined the roof and found nothing to indicate a bullet had passed through, and an Arthur Locker, who said he went to Bolinger's home and did what he could for him, bathing his face with wet cloths.

Locker said he asked Bolinger how his wound happened and Bolinger replied he "saw a funny light and heard a door slam." Bolinger also said something about trying to get to the telephone. Locker further testified he saw blood spots leading from the bed to the front door. While working with the injured man, he overheard a conversation between others present about the door being locked.

Bolinger's brother Bob stated he didn't see how anyone could get in since Fred always kept the door locked. Locker testified Fred Bolinger said something about the lock, but the defense was never able to clarify an exact statement as to exactly what the wounded man said on the subject.

Did they have to keep going over and over the same details? Walter admitted he was curious as to what had happened, but surely one or two people telling the same thing was enough. At this rate, the trial would take forever. He needed to get the last field plowed if he was going to be able to plant for spring.

The way these witnesses droned on and on...and the lawyers kept harping on the same questions had gotten to the point of being repulsive. Why couldn't these attorney types ask the question once and be done?

He personally didn't like hearing about all the violence and death. It made his mind get on thought trains he wanted to avoid. All this was enough to give a man bad dreams. As if he needed any more of those.

He gave a small, silent sigh.

The bonds of circumstantial evidence were further forged by testimonies of other witnesses who either saw Edmondson headed toward Bolinger's home the Sunday before the shooting, to earlier disputes the two men had over several years about many issues.

Testimony continued throughout Monday into Tuesday.

CHAPTER 3

Tuesday Judge Dolan called the first night session in the trial.

The main witness that evening was a Fred Fuston, who testified he was afraid of Edmondson. Fuston stated on the night of November 9th, he went to bed in the kitchen of his home, that during the night he slipped out of bed without his wife knowing it, put his clothes on outside, and met Will Edmondson and R. K. Mallett, another Edmondson friend.

According to Fuston, they all went to Fred Bolinger's home where Edmondson handed Fuston a pistol, the barrel pointed at him and told Fuston to take the gun, go inside, and kill Bolinger. Fuston said he refused and after a moment, Edmondson said "I will do it myself." Fuston said Edmondson went inside, they heard two shots, and Edmondson came out and announced "Well, I've killed him."

Fuston was cross-examined extensively as the defense attacked his story of slipping away from the room without his wife hearing him and other details. Fuston did become mixed up at times, but on the whole, maintained his original story.

Walter gave a real sigh, not caring who heard him. It had been a long and grueling day…sitting in the hard chairs while witness after witness droned on and on. Now they were into the evening. And still listening to descriptions over and over of the murder scene and the wounds and the blood evidence.

He shuddered, but not from cold. Distaste with the whole situation flooded his mind. He'd much rather be elsewhere.

With relief, he heard the jury dismissed for the night after being told not to discuss the case.

Walter hurried to the door. He could hardly wait to get home and see the family. Of course, the children would already be in bed. He hoped Dora had kept something hot to eat for him. The meal they'd fed the jury and called 'supper' wouldn't touch the tasty food his wife produced. Besides it was almost time for another pill. He'd need that tonight for sure.

He began the drive home. Details from the trial floated in and out of his brain. Stop! He needed to focus on something else. Something good and clean and wholesome.

He'd think about church. He loved listening to the reverend's powerful sermons. Sermons that really caused a man to take notice and examine himself about his life and how he lived it.

The sermon a couple of weeks ago, for instance. The pastor had talked about our relationship to God and what it should be. Inspiring was a weak word to describe the message and Walter's emotional response to it.

A response, that to some folks, probably seemed pretty silly. He could almost re-capture the sense of excitement that had swirled through him. A euphoria that made him want to respond to God with all he was...all he had.

He guessed some in the congregation thought him excessive since he'd gotten some funny looks when he tugged out his wallet and reverently placed it in the collection plate. Of course, the pastor had returned it after the service. Walter knew, though, a transaction and deeper commitment to God had taken place in him which was all he cared about.

He supposed no one would understand his murmured comment about "not needing this anymore," but he didn't care. He and God knew what he meant.

The lights of home shone ahead. He smiled in satisfaction. Thank God for home. He'd never survive if he had to be away from it for long.

Wednesday morning the first female witnesses were introduced and testified hearing Edmondson make remarks about "getting Bolinger out of the way," etc. during various conversations that took place in different homes. It was never determined if the remarks tended to strengthen the circumstantial chain of evidence or if they were merely comments made to impress listeners at the time.

Witnesses were also introduced giving testimony in attempts to destroy statements by Mrs. Fred Fuston.

She and Fuston were separated and she lived in Austin. She testified Edmondson came to her home, accompanied by his son-in–law, Aubrey Hoxie [Hopson], in September, 1930 and talked to her for about an hour and a half. Edmondson wanted her to swear Fred did not leave the room the night of the shooting, and that she knew he didn't.

Edmondson also wanted her to swear she had seen Bolinger's brothers give Fred money. Edmondson told her "the one who paid the truth and helped me out of this trouble would never suffer for anything as long as they lived."

The wife was pregnant, nervous and excited and was eventually excused by the defense without questioning after she said Edmondson wanted her to swear she did see him talk to Fred on the morning of November 9th, the day before Bolinger was shot.

She testified "If Fred left the room that night (November 9th) I did not know it," and "we slept in the same bed there in the kitchen."

Other witnesses were brought in to try to refute the testimony of Fuston, but only with varying degrees of success.

The prosecutor called W. T. Orman of San Saba, foreman of the grand jury which had indicted Edmondson, to try to make him testify proper procedure had not been followed, but the defense objected and the line of questioning was dropped.

The State rested its testimony.

The defense's motion requesting a verdict of acquittal was overruled by Judge Dolan.

The trial would continue.

CHAPTER 4

Preceding the introduction of the defense's testimony, defense attorney Gibb Calloway made a statement to the jury outlining what they intended to do.

They would attempt to prove Edmondson did not shoot Bolinger, that their land joined, and that a petition had been presented to the commissioner's court of San Saba county asking for permission for Edmondson and others who needed to reach the San Saba-Locker road to cross between places owned by Bolinger. The road would use only six miles of Bolinger's property.

He stated the defense would further show that Bolinger shot himself.

They would attempt to prove that with R. H. (R.K.) Mallett who took dinner with him the Sunday before, Edmondson walked across the pastures and fields to a rent house on the Bolinger farm to see about some furniture and implements he had bought, that they met a witness named Ghent and asked if he had seen Bolinger, since Edmondson wanted to see him about building a joint sheep-proof fence.

They would prove Edmondson did see Bolinger who agreed to it, and that the two, Edmondson and Mallett, agreed to go to San Saba the next day to see the commissioner's court about the road. When they did they found it had been agreed to, but the jury of view had failed to swear to their assessment of damages and that the court demanded this, so they took the papers and returned.

Further testimony would show that the morning the deceased was found shot, Edmondson and Mallett met and proceeded with arranging for the proper execution of the papers, seeing members of the jury on their way to San Saba where they heard of the Bolinger matter about twelve o'clock. They went on to San Saba where they were questioned by the sheriff.

Callaway stated the defense would seek to show further that Bolinger was an inoffensive man, peculiar, doubtful of those with whom he dealt, that he kept money at home because he feared banks, that Bolinger had various kinds of guns for its protection and that Edmondson had no desire to harm Bolinger since the road matter was completed and damages assessed in Bolinger's favor.

Numerous witnesses were introduced seeking to impeach witness Fred Fuston, all testifying his reputation for truthfulness was bad.

R. K. Mallett, an alleged accomplice of Edmondson, was originally indicted by the San Saba

County grand jury but was later dismissed. He testified he and Edmondson had never plotted Bolinger's death, that they had nothing against him.

Mallett vehemently denied the allegations at the end of the questioning by defense attorneys when they asked him "Did you and Edmondson go to the home of Fred Bolinger, and did Edmondson offer Fuston a gun and tell him to go kill old Bolinger, and he [Fuston] refused saying he had been raised better than that, that Edmondson said, "I will do it" and went in, did you hear two gunshots and did Edmondson come out of the house and say, "Well, the old ___, is dead." Did you walk away toward your homes across the fields and reaching [the] defendant's house leave without a word, later reaching your home, [where] you left without a word, and Fuston proceeded on toward his home, [with] not a word spoken from the time you left [Bolinger's place]?"

After all of the above interrogations, Mallett answered each, "No," and at the conclusion, "No, it is not true, we did not."

Cross-examination of the witness by District Attorney Hammond consumed more than an hour, as he again took him over all of the matters of which he had testified. The witness was questioned concerning every step he took from Sunday afternoon through Tuesday. He was questioned minutely why he and Edmondson had not returned to the Bolinger home to see about him.

The measurement of Edmondson and Mallett's shoes while they were in San Saba, Edmondson's failure to attend the funeral of Fred Bolinger, and other issues were gone over. The cross examination of the witness with such lines of questioning caused the defense counsel to appeal to the court for the injection of extraneous issues to be stopped. They were and the witness was excused.

Lawyers! They had gone on and on and on about events to the point where he could now recite them from memory. Enough was enough. It was unbelievable…all the scheming and underhanded stuff. People who were supposed to be friends. Couldn't tell from their testimony if they were or not. Sounded as though everybody had something against the victim.

Of course, Bolinger didn't sound exactly like a warm and friendly person either. But nobody deserved to be shot and left to die by himself. Still, the constant going over and over the same ground, trying to get the witnesses to say something different amounted to brow-beating in his opinion. Plus his brain was starting to overload with images he'd rather forget.

He crossed his arms. God, give me patience. How much longer would all the talking go on? It was fast approaching another not-so-delicious supper time and another evening session. At this rate, it would be another late night. And he'd forgotten to take his medication last night, he'd been so tired when he got home.

Oh, well, he probably didn't need it. He'd been doing pretty well lately. No reason to worry.

Following Mallett's testimony, seven citizens consisting of business men, farmers, and stockmen were introduced. They all testified they had known Mallett all his life, they knew his general reputation and his reputation for truth and veracity and all said it was good. Mallett's wife testified her husband did not leave the house that night.

Jake Chadwick, 41 years in San Saba, city marshal of San Saba, knew Fred Bolinger, also knew Will Edmondson for 30 years. About daylight on the 10th, he heard about Fred Bolinger being shot and he, the sheriff, constable, and justice of the peace went to Bolinger's home. They examined Bolinger, who was still alive. He had been shot under the left lower rib. They could feel the bullet upward near the skin on the right side, and thought it had ranged upward on a direct line.

They looked about the place, went to the cow-pen, followed some tracks by the pen to a crib. The tracks then came back. They covered them, later put Fred Bolinger's shoes in them and they fit. The tracks were probably why the other suspect's feet were measured at one point.

Later, with Joe Bolinger, a brother of Fred, and

another man, they searched quite a way around Bolinger's place and beyond, as did several other searchers for other tracks that might have been made by an intruder. No tracks were found.

The marshal testified he checked for firearms. There was a six-shooter on Bolinger's trousers on the floor at the head of the bed about sixteen or eighteen inches away. A Winchester was under Bolinger's pillow and a shotgun in the corner. They searched the bed clothes for powder burns and bullet holes, but found none.

He also testified he knew something about guns, had seen the bullet extracted from Bolinger and identified the missile. When he examined the gun, Chadwick found three loaded shells...two had been fired, the remaining three had been snapped (misfired). Three shells were exhibited. Chadwick picked out the two taken from the pistol.

A John Yates of Brownwood, formerly of San Saba, knew Fred Fuston at San Saba and had worked with him on city work. Yates had talked to Fuston about trading cars, but told Fuston he couldn't because he had to go to Llano. During their conversation, Yates said, "I wonder why Edmondson killed Mr. Bolinger?"

Fuston replied, "He did not kill him, was not there and knew nothing about it."

Yates asked "Why don't you tell the court that?

"Fuston said, 'the grand jury got him [Fuston]

scared and he did not know what he was swearing [to] and now if he told the court they would send him to the penitentiary.'"

On cross-examination, Yates could not give a very clear account of his own wanderings however, admitting he had lived briefly in many places.

The defense rested.

Tension tightened the muscles in Walter's neck and shoulders. The familiar beginning barbs of headache pain flashed through his temples. He massaged his neck, tried to be unobtrusive about it. Not a headache! Not now!

The ones he got resembled migraines...had ever since young adulthood. A headache could lay him low for a couple of days. He mustn't have one now. Who knew how much longer the trial would go on? He had to be able to hear the rest of the evidence...although by now, the repetition and constant changes in stories by witnesses, accusations by both slates of attorneys, made him want to scream.

How did someone survive serving on a jury in a trial so long and drawn out? As far as he was concerned, he'd make sure he never encountered another murder case...whether real or in a movie. The recurring nausea it caused, whether real or imaginary, only added to his mental discomfort.

He tried to concentrate again as another attorney asked the same witness more questions. Would this never end?

CHAPTER 5

Immediately after the defense rested, the State began the introduction of rebuttal testimony, introducing as their first witness, R.K. Mallett, a supposed accomplice of Edmondson's.

"Did you ask A. B. Spradling at Lake Victor to go on the witness stand and swear that he, Spradling, spent the night of November 9, 1925, with Will Edmondson?"

His answer was, "No, I did not."

Cross-examined, Mallett said he knew Mrs. Edmondson had testified in April, 1926, and before the grand jury that Will Edmonson owned a pistol.

Spradling testified he was a brother-in-law of Mallett and that Mallett had come to his home and asked him and his wife to help him and Will Edmondson out, presumably by testifying. Mrs. Spradling, a sister of Mallett's wife, was asked if this was true. She responded "Yes." Cross-examined, the witness could not remember what part of the year or time of day the conversation occurred.

Further witnesses again testified Fred Fuston's

reputation for truthfulness was bad.

Will Brown said he talked to Edmondson in October of 1925 who said "I will have that piece of land; if I can't buy it I will have it anyway." The testimony was excluded from the jury. Law enforcement officials from San Saba County testified several of the witnesses were known to not be truthful.

Further testimony finally concluded and Judge Dolan began preparation of the charge. It would reach the jury Thursday afternoon.

Three hours would then be allowed each side for final arguments. Then the case would go to the jury and a decision of guilty or not guilty would be proclaimed.

The jury received the case at 10:30 p.m. Thursday night.

Walter raised himself carefully from his seat in the jury box. Done at last. He grabbed a chair as dizziness swept over him. He dimly heard someone ask if he was all right. No. Maybe he should have taken his pills. He'd never felt like this before.

He motioned the other man forward, took careful steps to follow him down the courthouse corridor to the room where they would deliberate the case. Voices were babble – bits and pieces of sentences floated in and out of his brain.

"'Seventy-seven witnesses...didn't think we'd ever get through'....'That Fuston guy...what a piece of

work'...'wonder if we'll get out of here before morning?'"

Pressure radiated outward from his chest. Was he capable of making a right decision about Edmondson's guilt? He knuckled his temples, the headache pounded — a hundred hammers beat at his brain. Flashes of light came and went in his vision.

How would he know what was true or not? He couldn't even listen to the trial without getting sick. He didn't want to make any wrong decisions. After all, a man's life was at stake.

He continued to stagger along the hallway, practically bouncing from side wall to side wall. At last...the door.

Walter almost fell into the room. Voices assailed him from every direction. He could feel his eyes roll backward in his head as blackness descended throughout his brain, cancelling the flashes of light. Conscious thought faded.

He cried out as he felt himself fall.

****

"Somebody get a doctor."

"Stretch him out. He's all curled up in a ball."

Pandemonium reigned in the small room as men scurried around resembling ants swarming over a scrap of food. They ministered to the unconscious body before them in the best way they knew how.

A few moments later, a bailiff appeared in the doorway.

"What happened?"

"Dunno." The foreman swiped a forearm across his brow. *"Leschber here was staggering around, yelled out and fell. Isn't there a doc around somewhere?"*

"On the way." The bailiff gestured to the other men standing at one end of the confined space. *"You gents go on out. I'll wait here 'til the doc comes."*

"You sure?" The foreman sounded doubtful as to the propriety of their departure.

"Yep. Go on. He probably fainted. It was awful hot in there tonight."

The eleven men filed solemnly past Walter's prone body. Each gave him a doubtful glance.

"Don't look good to me," muttered one.

The bailiff gestured them out, reached forward and closed the door behind them. He took his own visual assessment of the fallen man, shook his head.

Walter was taken to his home where a doctor attended him. His wife, Dora, being a quiet, retiring woman unsure of what to do, called on a family member for help. Walter's younger brother, Reinhold, often acted as the unofficial head of the family.

A respected man in the community, he was known to do all he could to protect his family when he thought it was needed. The family allowed it since Reinhold knew all the right people in town and had a good reputation among them. Dora probably thought he would know what to do since she didn't.

Throughout the night the family waited and prayed. Walter continued to have episodes of consciousness alternated with more periods of blackout. When conscious, his shouts and ravings drew deep concern from Dora and Reinhold.

By morning, it was obvious Walter would not be returning to the jury room.

"What are we going to do?" Dora's question came out in a sob.

Reinhold gave her an awkward pat on the shoulder. "He's not himself, Dora. I know he has problems sometimes, but I've never seen him so bad. Was he taking his medication?"

"As far as I know. He'd been getting home so late...I'm not sure."

He nodded. "Doc thinks we need to take him to Austin and put him in the state hospital there for a while. Walt needs some treatment by somebody who knows how to deal with these things."

Dora's sobs reverberated in the small room.

Walter stirred.

Reinhold held up his hand. "Easy, Dora. Don't wake him. The sedative Doc gave him won't last much longer. I know it's hard, but pull yourself together. I've got to think...."

He paced the room once...twice...stopped before the distraught woman. "We've got to get him to Austin. That's the only chance he's got to get over...whatever this is." He cast a worried look at his older brother who lay stiff and silent.

"You...you really think it's necessary?"

"I do. I'll contact the judge and tell him Walter can't continue on the jury."

"But...but...if you tell him what's wrong, everybody will be talking. The children will hear...."

"I'll take care of it, Dora. Don't fret yourself. Get Walter ready as best you can. We'll get him into the car and I'll take him over to Austin. You can go see him in a day or two. Maybe by then he'll be better."

Dora swiped at her eyes, took a deep sniff. "All right. When do you want me to have him ready?"

"As quick as possible. I need to go to Judge Dolan's house after I make one stop." He patted her shoulder again. "Don't worry. It'll be okay."

Reinhold wheeled and left the room as Dora leaned over her unconscious husband and tenderly smoothed the hair away from his brow.

****

The door to the house opened abruptly. Judge Harry Dolan stood there, attired for another day in court.

"Reinhold. What brings you here? Is Walter okay?"

"Need to talk to you about that, Harry. You got a minute?"

"Sure." Dolan preceded the other man down the hall to an open doorway on the left. "Come in my office." He gestured toward a chair. "Have a seat."

Reinhold shook his head. "Can't stay but a minute.

I came to tell you Walter won't be able to continue on the jury. He's bad sick and can't even get out of bed."

"What's wrong with him?" Dolan's expression reflected a sudden thought. "He's not contagious, is he?"

"No. Nothing like that. To be honest, I think it's his mind. I'm going to take him to the mental hospital in Austin and see if they can treat him."

"That's too bad."

Dolan stood silent for a moment. "You know you can't just walk in and leave him at the hospital, don't you?"

"What do you mean? He's my brother and he needs help."

"Maybe so, but you have to have an order from me or a document signed by two physicians to commit him. I'll either have to issue the order or you'll need to wait for a day or two until the doctors can examine him."

"I can't do that. He's in bad shape. Whenever those drugs the doc gave him wear off, he's shoutin' about blood and murder and who knows what all. Dora and the kids can't have him around doing that."

Reinhold paused, pondered. "You can sign a paper to allow me to take him in?"

"Yep. There's a special order that'll allow you to do it rather than a sheriff."

"I guess that's what we need to do. I'm sorry, Harry. If there was any other way...."

Dolan shrugged and gave a half smile. "What they pay me for, Reinhold. What they pay me for."

He stood, as though waiting for a further response. After a brief pause, he pulled open a drawer in the desk, thumbed through some papers. "Here. I'll sign the order and you can take Walter today."

"Thanks. The family and I appreciate it."

Dolan nodded. "Guess I'll have to declare a mistrial and start over."

"I wish it could be different, Harry."

"Not a problem."

Reinhold reached inside the briefcase he carried, paused before withdrawing his hand.

"One thing."

"What's that?"

"I'd appreciate it if you could say Walter can't continue on the jury because he was took sick...without any details. I don't want to make things hard for Dora and the kids by people gossiping and all."

Dolan looked thoughtful. "I can see that."

Reinhold withdrew his hand from inside the briefcase. He held a bottle of Scotch. He carefully sat the offering on Dolan's desk.

"It'd be much appreciated."

Dolan picked up the bottle, inspected the label, gave a nod. "Don't worry. I'll take care of it. And I'll take care of the copy of the order now."

He tore off the duplicate page of the form he'd signed, handed the original to Leschber, wadded the copy and tossed it into a wastebasket by the desk.

"Much obliged."

"Anytime, Reinhold." He patted the bottle.

"Anytime."

According to a newspaper account, the jury in the Will Edmondson murder trial was discharged Friday morning, February 6, 1931, at 10:30 a.m., twelve hours after receiving the case at 10:30 p.m. Thursday night.

The court entry stated:

"The defendant and his counsel were brought into court and received the following report: That one of the jurors is critically ill and that they could not agree on a verdict. Mistrial is ordered and entered and cause continued for term."

The article further stated, "The illness of Mr. Leschber was reported to have manifested itself Thursday night, and his condition was stated to have become so alarming that the discharge of the jury at once was necessary, whereupon Judge Dolan ordered and the twelve men were discharged.

"The case had consumed the entire week, including night sessions, during which time seventy-seven witnesses were placed on the stand. This was the fifth trial of the case."

CHAPTER 6

Reinhold drove carefully, gave an occasional quick glance sideways to where Walter lolled against the passenger side door.

His concern deepened as his brother seemed to be coming out of the drug-induced fog the doctor's medication had put him in. He hoped Walter wouldn't awaken until they got to the hospital. Trying to drive and tend a man not in his right mind would be a challenge.

The stress of being awake all night and his brother's alarming state of mind and body, placed him under a strain almost too much to bear. He felt the load of care for Walter's wife, Dora, and the four children press upon him, with the fifth to arrive soon.

He drew a deep breath. He'd do what he could...the best he could...to see Walter got the help he needed, and take care of his brother's family. Perhaps a time of confinement would bring Walter to his senses and he'd be able to be dismissed soon.

The sound of a horn behind him jerked him out of his introspection.

Good thing somebody was impatient. He'd almost missed the turn into the hospital grounds.

Reinhold signaled a right turn. A sign reading "Austin State Hospital" identified the place.

He pulled beneath the portico labeled "Admissions" and stopped the car.

Reinhold pulled open the door and walked inside. He needed to move quickly before Walter came to. A counter ran across one end of a medium-sized room. A woman sat behind it, typing.

When she saw him, she rose and came forward.

"May I help you?"

The next hour assumed the proportions of a nightmare as Walter was admitted, helped inside, and taken to a room.

Reinhold hated walking the hallway that led to his brother's confinement. The room where they put Walter was small with only a cot inside.

The orderly helped Walter lie down, stepped away. "I'll wait outside."

Reinhold nodded, stood staring at his brother until the door closed. He gazed around the room. Walter was going to hate being here. He'd never liked being shut up in small spaces. Hopefully the doctors could help him and Walter could go home soon.

He heaved a sigh, reached out and grasped Walter's shoulder. "I'll be back, brother. God bless."

He squeezed, turned and walked to the door.

The still figure behind him didn't resemble his brother. Reinhold could only hope it would be a short stay.

Unfortunately, Walter's confinement lasted almost

six weeks. On Thursday, March 19, 1931, he took matters into his own hands.

Walter shook his head, tried to clear the grogginess from his brain. He hated what the drugs they gave him did to his mind. They'd doubled his normal medication, leaving him fuzzy and unsteady. He hated worse some of the other treatments they'd performed.

He shuddered at the memory of being strapped to a table and electric shocks sent through him. They told him it would make him better...the treatment and the drugs...but he couldn't see it yet.

Worse was not being at home, not seeing his family. Oh, Dora had visited him a couple of times, but he'd been so fogged in his mind he almost didn't recognize her. Her visits had both ended in tears and a panic-stricken expression on her face as though she didn't know him anymore.

He missed the children, too. And his farm. Being outdoors planting or reaping. What wouldn't he give to be there now?

Would he ever be able to leave this place? It had been weeks...weeks since his confinement. He'd thought perhaps the dreams and visions of blood and guns and shooting would leave his mind in time, but they only grew more vivid every day...torturing his waking moments...at least the ones where he had some grasp of reality

Talking to the doctor hadn't helped either. Nothing seemed to help anymore.

He struggled to a sitting position. Almost time for more medicine. He'd come to hate the sight of the attendants. Perhaps they thought they were helping him, but they weren't. If he had to stay here for more days…weeks…. He refused to think beyond that.

His lips firmed in decision…he wasn't going to let them keep him here any longer. No matter what he had to do, he would get away. Whatever it took, he would do…even if he had to end his own life. After all, he was as good as dead now…perhaps if he were truly dead, he would no longer be a burden and embarrassment to his family.

He cringed when he thought of the gossip that must be circulating in his hometown. At the church. Surely Reinhold, no matter how much influence he had, hadn't been able to keep Walter's whereabouts from people. And what had they told the children? Where did they think Daddy had gone?

A sob tore its way from his throat. He clenched and unclenched his fists. He had to do something…he had to.

The metallic clank of a key being inserted in the lock returned him to the moment. He wasn't going to take any more of their pills. He was smart. He would figure a way to get out of here and go home.

Walter slumped, assumed a stupefied expression, let his mouth droop half open.

The sound of footsteps assured him the attendant approached the cot.

"Here you are. Open wide."

Two pills dropped into his mouth.

"Swallow."

Walter shoved the pills to one side under his tongue, made a swallowing motion.

"Good boy. I'll come check on you in a few minutes."

The attendant's half-sneering tone made Walter want to hit him, but he forced himself to remain still.

Retreating footsteps, the metallic clang of a door closing, told Walter the man had gone.

He swung his legs slowly around to the edge of the cot and struggled into a sitting position.

He spat the pills onto the floor and toed them out of sight. He had to get out of here…now. He had only moments before the attendant would return.

A quick survey of the room showed him nothing he could use as a means of exit. The one window in the room was barred. No hope he could get out that way. Was there any way to escape?

His gaze dropped to the cot where he sat. He stared at the two thin sheets that served as linens.

The horrible plan burst into his mind full-blown.

They would never let him leave this place. The only way of escape for him would be death.

He heaved a sigh. Very well, then. If it was the only way…. A deep gulp, then determination took over.

He stood, ripped the sheets from the bed, tied a quick knot between the two. Jumbling them into a bundle, he stuffed it under one arm, tiptoed to the door and tested the handle.

Unlocked as usual until the attendant returned to

make his final check for the night.

Walter eased out of the room, pulled the door until it almost latched. He couldn't afford the noise pulling it completely shut would make.

Where to go? It had to be fast or he'd be stopped. That must not happen.

He stole quietly along the hall in the opposite direction from where the attendant medicated other inmates.

The doorway leading to an outside corridor beckoned. He gently tested it. Locked! He spied a door standing half open a few steps further down the hallway. He made his way there. A flight of stairs.

Casting a quick look around, he pushed the door open a bit more, shrinking as a metallic scrape resounded. Without further hesitation, he headed toward the staircase.

Up. He needed to go up. Get higher to do what he had to do.

Another flight and a second door faced him. A key protruded from the lock. What did the stenciled letters say?

Roof. Yes, the roof. It should be high enough.

He shoved through the doorway, panting under the burden of the thin sheets that sufficed for those confined. He was weaker than he'd thought.

No matter. He had to leave. Regardless of what he had to do. No more blood. No more questions and answers. No more voices accusing…defending.

The moonlit sky provided a searchlight-like brilliance to the rooftop.

Then he saw them. Pipes. Pipes sticking out of the roof. Perhaps they would be strong enough to hold his weight. It wouldn't take long.

He walked to the pipe closest to the edge of the roof and tested it. It would do.

A quick knot tied one end of the sheets to the pipe. He pulled. The knot held. Now for himself.

He walked to the edge of the roof and peered down…shrank back. He'd never liked heights. Three stories up made his brain swim.

The drums started again in his head…the voices grew louder and louder in his mind. He tied the free end of the sheet around his neck and sat on the roof edge.

Don't look down.

A brief moment of sanity scrolled the faces of his wife, his children, across his memory.

"I'm sorry," he gasped.

He glanced toward the heavens.

"Forgive me."

He scooted forward and launched himself from the roof.

Walter's body was discovered late that night. It took four firemen and a ladder truck to retrieve him from where he hung against the building.

Walter Leschber had made his escape.

CHAPTER 7

The telephone rang once, twice.

Reinhold Leschber fought his way to consciousness, fumbled for the receiver.

"Hello?"

A chill swept over him as he listened to the voice on the other end of the line. Disbelief caused him only to process bits and pieces of the words.

"Your brother…the roof…identify…."

Now he was completely awake as the horror of what he'd heard became reality.

Walter!

An hour later, he entered the doorway of the building where Walter had been confined.

A uniformed attendant acknowledged his arrival, went to a door and tapped, stuck his head inside, spoke, turned around.

"Mr. Preston will be right with you."

The next hour would live forever in Reinhold's memory. The process of identifying the body, signing the necessary papers, gathering the few belongings Walter had at the hospital.

Reinhold went through most of it in a fog. Until Preston asked his final question.

"Where should the body be sent?"

His mind cleared in an instant, went into overdrive.

The body. Of course, there would have to be a funeral. But how could they have one when everybody in town thought Walter had been away on business for six weeks?

And suicide. There would be no way the pastor would allow Walter to be buried in the church cemetery. The Lutheran church didn't allow suicides to be buried in hallowed ground in this day and time.

"Of course," Preston's voice reclaimed his attention, "if you don't have a place, we do have a potter's field where our...inmates without families or identities are buried. Is that the case here?"

Reinhold's mind raced through possibilities and scenarios. He had to protect the family and its name. Dora and the children, too. He needed to talk to Dora. What would she be willing to do? To say or not say?

"I'll get back to you later today." He turned and hurried out the door. Perhaps the long drive to Williamson County would give him the correct answer.

After all, he was the protector and guardian of the family name. He had to be.

Funeral services were held at 2:00 p.m. on Thursday, March 20, 1931 for Walter Leschber at the Lutheran church in Walburg. The newspaper obituary stated only that his death occurred in a hospital in Austin at 10:30 p.m. on the preceding Tuesday evening. Rev. H. Sieck, pastor of the Lutheran church, of which the deceased was a member, conducted the services. The Friedrich Funeral Home, Georgetown, was in charge of the funeral details.

The deceased was survived by his wife, four children, his parents, and three brothers and three sisters.

On May 1st Walter Leschber would have been 37 years old.

****

What made Walter Leschber's death unusual?

For one thing, there is no official record he was ever admitted to the Austin State Hospital for observation or treatment. Only a story told and repeated by one now deceased who claimed to know the particulars of the case.

The records for admittances, deaths, inquests, etc. are held by the Austin State Hospital as confidential. An Open Records request, by a descendant of Walter's, was not granted due to the permanent confidentiality of the hospital's files.

There is no record in Williamson or Travis counties of an inquest being conducted or an autopsy being performed. No death certificate was ever issued by any city, county, or private physician. At least not one ever discovered or mentioned in available records.

There is no record in any of the county files of any

emergency commitment signed by Judge Dolan. Of course, that could have been dealt with as detailed in the previously fictionalized scene between Dolan and Reinhold.

So there are questions remaining. And others, as well.

Since during the early 30's, the Lutheran church did not allow suicides to be buried in a church cemetery, the question has to be raised. Was Walter's body actually in the casket buried in the Zion Lutheran Church cemetery?

If the pastor had known Walter was a suicide, would he have conducted the service? Interestingly enough, there is no official note in the church records showing Walter was buried there. Is that meaningful, or merely an administrative oversight?

Or perhaps was Walter really buried in the potter's field cemetery attached to the Austin State Hospital under a different name, or anonymously, and an empty casket buried in the church graveyard to keep scandal from the family (mental illness would have been considered a scandal in 1931) or to satisfy church rules which existed at the time?

Did Reinhold protect the family to the extent he managed every detail of whatever was done and never told anyone or left any records about it in his own papers?

The gravesite for Walter Leschber is now located in the center of the church cemetery not far from the fence. Suicides in those days could be buried outside the fenced part of the cemetery. Was Walter buried there, and over time, as fence boundaries changed, did his grave location wind up in the cemetery proper?

Many unanswered questions abound, but ones which, after eighty-three years, can't be totally verified through existing records, agencies, or people.

****

What about the Will Edmondson trial that probably triggered Walter's death? Was it ever resolved?

The *Williamson County Sun* reported the sixth trial of Will Edmondson, San Saba County rancher and farmer, was called at 10:00 o'clock on Monday morning, March 16, 1931 in 26th District Court, Judge Harry Dolan presiding. Formalities were quickly taken care of and both sides announced "ready for trial" immediately when the case was called.

The work of selecting a jury was begun and by noon four had been secured. The examination of prospective jurors indicated the State desired to dispose of the trial, as prospective jurors were not questioned this time concerning their "conscientious scruples against inflicting the death penalty." Obviously the State didn't expect to secure a death verdict in the case anymore.

The five trials cost Edmondson a fortune and the case cost the State possibly above sixty thousand dollars, a lot of money in 1931. Prosecution and defense alike appeared to be worn and tired of the situation.

The last juror for the trial was secured at 4:30 p.m. Monday afternoon and the court adjourned until 7:30 p.m., announcing night sessions would be held and the case rushed to completion during the current week.

George Padier, Blanco County Indian (a newcomer to the proceedings), and Fred Fuston (again) supplied the bulk of the evidence for the prosecution. Padier testified Edmondson had offered him $500 and a farm to slay Bolinger. Fuston said he went to Bolinger's house with Edmondson and the rancher handed him a gun and asked him to kill Bolinger.

Padier and Fuston both testified they refused. Fuston said after he refused to do the shooting Edmondson himself took the gun and went into the Bolinger home. Fuston said a few minutes later, he heard two shots and Edmondson returned and said "he is dead."

The case was expected to reach the jury Friday or Saturday.

On March 31, 1931, the *Williamson County Sun* reported Will Edmondson, tried for the sixth time for the slaying of Fred Bolinger, was acquitted.

So what did finally happen to Edmondson after all those trials? A couple of months after he was acquitted, he and his son-in-law, Aubrey Hopson, were in a horse-pulled wagon on the way back from Brownwood, Texas, when an argument ensued and Will Edmondson was fatally shot.

No charges were brought against Hopson, as the family supposedly did not have the energy to follow through with any more court trials. According to a great-grandson, nothing has ever been spoken of in the family about why Will Edmondson was shot by Hopson, although they all have their theories.

****

After eighty-three years, many questions remain unanswered about what actually happened to Walter Leschber.

An unproved theory mentioned by a Leschber family member was that Walter had been poisoned. Interestingly, when the case was described to a former court employee who served for a number of years in another county, their immediate response was, "He was poisoned."

Evidently in earlier days, poisoning a juror must have been a favorite method of forcing a mistrial. Could this have been what happened to Walter? But why would a mistrial have been necessary? Edmondson could still be tried again, as later happened. There would have been no point in such an event to cause that to happen.

One of Walter's sisters, interviewed in a nursing home prior to her death, stated Walter had an aneurysm. That, of course, could account for his symptoms, but when available information was reviewed, it was discovered Walter's father died from an aneurysm. Perhaps the woman's comment stemmed from confusion or from a desire to find a more acceptable answer than suicide.

Another family member heard, second-hand, that Walter had been drugged (for some unknown reason) while on the jury and had been taken by Reinhold and Walter's father to an institution in Austin where the Brown School, near the intersection of North Loop and Burnet Road, was later located. The El Presidente Apartments now occupy the space. The building where Walter was supposedly taken in 1931, was described as a large, white farmhouse (probably also used initially by the Brown School when it was founded in 1940).

She had been told by Reinhold Leschber that Walter died there from the drugging. Unless Walter was allergic to whatever he had been given (and why would he have been drugged anyway?) it's unknown how a drug could have killed him. Another variation mentioned is that all of the jury was drugged, but only Walter had a bad reaction. There is no record that any such crime was ever reported or investigated by the authorities, nor that the judge knew of any such incident. Telling the story to his descendent may have been simply another attempt by Reinhold to save face for the family rather than admitting to a suicide.

It is unusual, however, in that Reinhold, while visiting the family member in the early 40's, went for a walk in the neighborhood, and came back and reported that he'd seen the location where 'they' took Walter that night.

The relative felt that Walter and Reinhold's father could have been part of that trip since the father was known to finance things for family members when needed, but that is not definite either. Her assumption is that Walter was brought to the facility in Austin since he couldn't be treated for whatever reasons in either Georgetown or Round Rock. There is no way, of course, to verify this theory since no records exist.

A number of questions also remain about what actually caused Walter's apparent breakdown, if that was indeed what happened. The symptoms described are common in bipolar disorder. But, they could also be descriptive of an aneurysm or even another mental or physical condition not previously considered. Two of Walter's relatives said he 'went berserk' and 'went insane.'

Without a death certificate ever being issued (or at least ever being found in either Travis or Williamson counties) it is impossible to ascertain if there were underlying physical/mental conditions that could have led to Walter's demise.

Suicide or natural causes? No one really knows. But it was definitely an unusual death in many respects.

Unfortunately, today the story of Walter Leschber has few definitive answers, but the truth perhaps could still surface in the future.

ADDENDUM

I chose to use bipolar disorder as Walter's means of breakdown after researching possible illnesses and talking to various sources familiar with the story.

For the reader's information, the following facts may be of interest.

BIPOLAR DISORDER

[From Brain & Behavior Research Foundation website]

Bipolar disorder, formerly known as manic-depressive illness, is a brain and behavior disorder characterized by severe shifts in a person's mood and energy, making it difficult for the person to function. More than 5.7 million American adults, or 2.6 percent of the population age 18 or older, in any given year have bipolar disorder.

The condition typically starts in late adolescence or early adulthood, although it can show up in children and in older adults. People often live with the disorder without having it properly diagnosed and treated.

Bipolar disorder causes repeated mood swings, or episodes, that can make someone feel very high (mania) or very low (depressive). The cyclic episodes are punctuated by normal moods.

Bipolar disorder cannot yet be diagnosed physiologically by blood tests or brain scans. Currently, diagnosis is based on symptoms, course of illness, and family history. Clinicians rule out other medical conditions, such as a brain tumor, stroke or other neuropsychiatric illnesses that may also cause mood disturbance. The different types of bipolar disorder are diagnosed based on the pattern and severity of manic and depressive episodes.

While no cure exists for bipolar disorder, it is treatable and manageable with psychotherapy and medications. Bipolar disorder is much better controlled when treatment is continuous. Mood changes can occur even during treatment.

BRAIN ANEURYSMS

[From Mayo Clinic website]

A brain aneurysm is a bulging, weak area in the wall of an artery that supplies blood to the brain. In most cases, it causes no symptoms and goes unnoticed. In rare cases it ruptures, causing a stroke.

A person may inherit the tendency to form aneurysms, or they may develop because of the hardening of the arteries and aging. Most brain aneurysms cause no symptoms and may only be discovered during tests for another, usually unrelated, condition.

In other cases, an unruptured aneurysm will cause problems by pressing on areas in the brain. When this happens, the person may suffer from severe headaches, blurred vision, changes in speech, and neck pain, depending on what areas of the brain are affected and how bad the aneurysm is.

AUSTIN STATE HOSPITAL

[From Texas Department of State Health Services – Austin State Hospital website]

The Austin State Hospital (ASH) is one of eleven inpatient facilities within the Texas Department of State Health Services system.

The hospital's inpatient treatment programs are responsible for delivery of a broad array of mental health services to a 3,094,115 person, 38-county service area located in South Central Texas.

Formerly the Texas State Lunatic Asylum, the original hospital building houses the administrative staff of ASH. It is the third oldest standing public building in Texas.

The lunatic asylum, renamed the Austin State Hospital in 1925, strived to offer patients the most modern treatments, including art, music, and recreational therapy.

It also provided state-of-the-art medical care, such as psychiatric drugs, hydrotherapy, electroconvulsive shock treatment, and on rare occasions, surgical lobotomy.

The original building, which was dressed up with a classical portico in 1904, offered three stories and a basement for administrative offices and staff and patient quarters. Its thick, hard plaster walls could endure frequent scrubbing and the thick limestone walls and high ceilings offered relief from the Texas heat.

Noisy patients were separated from quiet ones, and all patients lived above ground in rooms with at least one window. As the patient population grew from the initial twelve patients to nearly 700 by the late 1890's, additional wings and buildings sprang up.

The asylum functioned as a self-supporting village with artesian wells, gardens, a dairy, ice factory, and a sewing/tailor shop. These other historic buildings were eventually destroyed by fire or demolished to make way for newer buildings.

The Austin State Hospital, which once housed more than 3,000 patients during the 1960's, currently serves as an acute care facility for its 300 patients. Patients typically stay several days to a few weeks until their condition stabilizes and they can return to their communities.

The focus of treatment is stabilization of acute psychiatric illnesses and return to the community where outpatient support services can be provided by the community centers that work with ASH.

ABOUT THE AUTHOR

D. A. Featherling writes in multiple genres. She has penned mysteries, romantic comedies, millennial fiction, and romance. She has written a non-fiction cold case murder title as well. Her administrative years in corporations, state agencies, and a university physics research center, and as owner of her own home staging business, make her an ideal candidate to write about the lives and loves of a variety of people and professions.

She has also written numerous non-fiction and technical pieces and has won awards for journalism, fiction, and public speaking.

D. A. co-founded the CenTex Chapter of the American Christian Fiction Writers (ACFW) and has served as President and Vice-President. She is a member of several other writers' groups as well.

She lives in Georgetown, Texas and appears and/or speaks at events for civic organizations, clubs, churches, and schools upon request.

For speaking engagements or book signings:
D. A. Featherling
512-663-1407 or
dafeatherling@gmail.com

Website: *www.dafeatherling.com*

OTHER BOOKS
BY
D. A. FEATHERLING

Mysteries

It Adds Up to Murder (**It's Murder at the Office Series**)

Murder Outside the Box (**Staged for Murder Series**)

Romantic Comedies

Sauce for the Goose
Kissing Frogs
Double Trouble
Making Over Caro

Millennial Fiction

Time Out
Double Time

Non-Fiction

Who Killed Ben Miller &
Death of a Juror

Last Time

— Book 3 —
Out of Time Series

When time itself is running out…where can they go?

Coming — 2015

D. A. Featherling
~ "Fiction a la carte" ~

Made in the USA
Monee, IL
24 February 2020

22191306R00096